a *perfect* day
for a *picnic*

a *perfect* day
for a *picnic*

*Over **80** recipes for outdoor feasts
to share with family and friends*

Tori Finch

Photography by
Georgia Glynn-Smith

LONDON • NEW YORK

This book is for Ned

Senior Designer Barbara Zuñiga
Editor Rebecca Woods
Production Gordana Simakovic
Art Director Leslie Harrington
Editorial Director Julia Charles

Food Stylist Rosie Reynolds
Prop Stylist Liz Belton
Indexer Hilary Bird

First published in 2013 by
Ryland Peters & Small
20–21 Jockey's Fields
London WC1R 4BW
and
Ryland Peters & Small, Inc.
519 Broadway, 5th Floor
New York NY10012
www.rylandpeters.com

10 9 8 7 6 5 4 3 2

Text © Tori Finch 2013
Design and photographs © Ryland, Peters & Small 2013

ISBN: 978 1 84975 353 1

A catalogue record for this book
is available from the British Library.

A CIP record for this book is available
from the Library of Congress.

Printed and bound in China.

Notes

* All spoon measurements are level, unless otherwise
  stated.

* Eggs are medium (UK) or large (US) unless otherwise
  specified. Uncooked or partially cooked eggs should not
  be served to the very old, frail, young children, pregnant
  women or those with compromised immune systems.

* When a recipe calls for the grated zest of lemons or limes
  or uses slices of fruit, buy unwaxed fruit and wash well
  before using. If you can only find treated fruit, scrub well
  in warm soapy water before using.

* Ovens should be preheated to the specifed temperature.
  Recipes in this book were tested in a regular oven. If using
  a fan-assisted oven, follow the manufacturer's instructions
  for adjusting temperatures.

Contents

Introduction

There is something hugely nostalgic about eating in the open air. Just the thought of an idyllic setting, a large comfortable rug, perhaps your favourite book and an array of delectable bites is heavenly. For what is better than eating alfresco on a warm balmy day? Under vast open skies and with rolling hills, a windswept beach, a mountain stream or wooded parkland as your stage, a picnic has the ability to take all one's cares away and let the great outdoors, food in our bellies and excellent company fill us with warmth and happiness.

As a child I spent summers down at the beach with my family. Memories come flooding back when I think of those special times: the sounds from the nearby amusement park; the smell of sea air mingled with fish and chips; soft ice cream with a soggy chocolate flake; but most of all, I remember the anticipation of discovering what was for lunch. My mother had been busy preparing mouthwatering treats all morning. The kitchen would be filled with delicious aromas, like quiche straight out of the oven, or that mouthwatering smell of cookie dough rising. We would all jump in the car with a motley collection of baskets and bags, buckets and spades, towels and wind breaks and all the provisions needed for a perfect picnic. Now I close my eyes, the sun dapples through and I go back to the memories of those wonderful days. Picnics are quintessentially associated with happy times – they represent an escape from the daily grind and a chance to let down your hair.

Where the word picnic derived from no-one can be sure. It could be old English for 'pot luck' where all attending would bring a dish, or the word may be derived from French *piquer* 'to pick' and *nique*, on 'a thing of little importance', although I'd be hard pushed to say a flaky meat pie was of little importance! One thing is for sure, the art of picnicking is long established and much loved.

The joy of eating outdoors is that it can be as simple or as glamorous as you like. While organizing a picnic on a grand scale is about delegation and organization, a rustic picnic can be equally as wonderful, with just a blanket or two, some jam sandwiches, and of course some good company to share them with. The most wonderful thing about picnicking is there are few rules, you can go as wild or as tame as you like. Either way, just packing a hamper full of things you have made to share with the people whose company you most enjoy is delicious in itself and if you stick to a theme and use savvy ways to transport and present your picnic, it needn't be a headache.

This book is a tribute to the picnic in all its forms, be it a family day at the beach, a trip out in the car to your favourite wild spot with a flask of tea and a hunk of cake, or a cheerful children's party. A picnic is one of life's simple pleasures – they are about relaxing in the great outdoors, for seeing our children run with abandonment whilst stuffing down a sausage roll. Mostly, they are a way of appreciating the good things in life. Live. Love. Picnic. Of course, one of the most important factors of a picnic is the feast – whether you are preparing an intimate picnic for two or a gathering of ten, within these pages you will find themes, recipes and inspirations for any alfresco occasion.

Planning Your Picnic

I think, as with most things, if you plan your picnic well, you are in for success. Picnics should, for the most part, be informal gatherings, but even the simplest of picnics will benefit from a little bit of forethought.

First and foremost, find your idyllic picnic location. This can be the rolling countryside, a city park, a windswept beach, a wooded glade, beside a beautiful river or anywhere else with a pleasing outlook. Check it out first. A place you once visited years ago may have changed and it would be most disappointing to reach the destination in mind and find a great sprawling superstore in situ. Check suitability for all those involved. Of course, an idealistic spot by a large river sounds divine, but if there are young children with you, will you need eyes in the back of your head? Perhaps a wide open country park would suit better?

The next step is choosing a theme. Listed in this book are a number of themes to choose from. They range from a rustic French feast or exotic Middle Eastern-inspired picnic, to a romantic getaway or luxury extravaganza for a truly special occasion. And I could have added dozens more: a foraging picnic, perfect for a crisp autumn morning after the rains, including wild mushroom picking and hunting bushes and trees for nuts and berries. Or how about a breakfast picnic? Take a skillet on an early morning walk and set up a camp fire to cook breakfast. (See page 48 for more help on Choosing Your Menu.)

Check out the weather a few days before and again on the day. Online weather reports are best, which can give you an hour by hour account if the sunshine seems a little haphazard. Even if the forecast doesn't show sun all day, don't despair, it doesn't mean your picnic will be a wash out – simply get prepared with a gazebo or take extra sweaters to pop on when the sun goes behind the clouds.

Or you could warm up with a game. Think ahead and try to incorporate other activities around the picnic, such as a ramble or hike or outdoor games. Frisbee is always a fun option and obviously a frisbee is light and easy to carry. Other ideas could be a game of rounders, baseball or cricket, hide and seek is great for the Teddy Bears' Picnic, and how about hosting a sand-castle building competition if your heading to the beach for the day?

Before you leave, plan your route if the location is some way away, making sure you get there in plenty of time so you can enjoy the surroundings. And if you plan on having a wee tipple, make sure you designate a driver to get you home safely.

When preparing the picnic think about what you can make in advance to save time on the day. While salads and desserts often need to be made on the day, pies and cakes can be prepared a day or two before. And if you are really pushed for time, opt for a barbecue so you can simply make a marinade and salad beforehand and prepare the rest of the meal on site over hot coals.

Become a list-ologist and jot down all the food, drinks and accessories you need to take. Tick off as you go and use savvy ways to store and transport the food and any other items (I go into this further in Packing Your Picnic on page 86).

Lastly, when you get to the destination and set up the feast, don't forget to relax, take your shoes off, enjoy the moment and pour yourself a large glass – you deserve it.

1 Vintage Garden Party

A warm day is a perfect excuse for a picnic. Set up a trestle table in a shady spot in the garden, lay it with pretty vintage tablecloths, odd chairs from around the house and any bits of china you have lying around. This is relaxed, informal dining at its best, and is magical shared with family and friends. As the sun sets in the west, light candles and tealights in jam jars and enjoy the feast into the balmy evening. These recipes are great for transporting from kitchen to table, but if you are out and about for your picnic, then most of these recipes can be transported and are delicious eaten cold, too.

Crostini Two Ways

This recipe makes a great starter or nibble to put out before the feast begins. All of the elements are perfect for transporting in separate containers. The toasted crostini can be made a few days before and kept in an airtight container. When it comes to serving, pile a crostini high with the beans or the salsa verde and feta, or, for a great flavour combustion, combine the two toppings. I sometimes serve a larger portion of the beans as a salad and the salsa verde works amazingly well dolloped onto a sheet of puff pasty and baked similarly to the mozzarella tart recipe on page 18.

To make the crostini, preheat the oven to 220°C (425°F) Gas 7.

Brush both sides of each baguette slice with plenty of olive oil. Arrange the baguette slices on a baking sheet, scatter the garlic slices and thyme sprigs over the tops and bake in the preheated oven for about 10 minutes, until the bread is golden and the edges are crisp. Allow to cool on a wire rack before serving with one or both of the toppings below.

1 baguette, sliced on the bias into
½-cm/¼-inch thick slices
60 ml/¼ cup olive oil
3 garlic cloves, thinly sliced
4 sprigs of fresh thyme

serves 6

Flageolet Beans with Chilli & Lemon

Tip the beans into a sieve/strainer and rinse thoroughly under cold, running water. Allow to drain and dry a little before transferring to a mixing bowl. Add the olive oil, lemon juice, chilli and garlic, season well with salt and pepper and toss the beans in the dressing to coat.

To serve, spoon onto a crostini slice and enjoy.

1 x 410-g/14-oz. can flageolet beans
3 tablespoons virgin olive oil
freshly squeezed juice of 2 lemons
1 red chilli, deseeded and finely
chopped
1 garlic clove, crushed
sea salt and ground black pepper

Salsa Verde with Feta

In a mortar and with a pestle (or in a food processor, blending only briefly so that the mixture is still chunky) crush the garlic, then add the anchovy fillets and crush again to make a rough paste. Add the shallot and lemon zest, give it a good bash with the pestle and mix well. You should get lovely wafts of the flavours combining together.

Stir in the capers, herbs and lemon juice, bruising the herbs a little with the pestle but certainly not pounding to a purée. Season to taste with salt and pepper and add enough olive oil to get the consistency you want – I usually find 1–2 tablespoons is enough.

Crumble in the feta and mix before serving with the crostini slices.

1 garlic clove
4 anchovy fillets
1 shallot, finely chopped
freshly squeezed juice and grated
zest of 1 lemon
2 tablespoon capers, rinsed and
drained, chopped if large
a bunch of fresh parsley, roughly
chopped
a bunch of fresh oregano, roughly
chopped
½ bunch of fresh mint, roughly
chopped
olive oil, to taste
200 g/7 oz. feta cheese
sea salt and ground black pepper

750 g/1½ lb. Jersey royal new
potatoes, washed and left whole
750 g/1½ lb. fresh broad/fava beans,
shelled
750 g/1½ lb. fresh peas, shelled
500 g/1 lb. mangetout/snow peas,
trimmed
1 bunch of fresh flatleaf parsley,
roughly chopped
2 tablespoons chopped fresh mint
180 g/6 oz. cooked ham hock meat,
shredded
70 g/2 big handfuls of pea shoots,
to garnish (optional)
sea salt and ground black pepper

For the creamy mustard dressing:
3 tablespoons extra virgin olive oil
3 tablespoons white wine vinegar
a good pinch of sea salt
1 generous teaspoon French
wholegrain mustard
2 teaspoons crème fraîche
1 banana shallot (or two small
shallots) very finely diced

serves 4–6

Ham Hock, Bean & Mint Salad with a Creamy Mustard Dressing

Ham hock, broad/fava beans, mint and mustard are a marriage made in flavour heaven and this salad is summer served on a plate. If you are making this to take out on a picnic, I find it is best to keep the ham hock, herbs and pea shoots separate from the dressing until just before serving, as the herbs and shoots tend to wilt. Keep the two elements in separate containers, then combine when ready to serve.

Bring a large saucepan of water to the boil, add the new potatoes and boil for 15–20 minutes until cooked through. Remove from heat, drain and leave to cool.

Add more water to the pan, bring to the boil again, then add the broad/fava beans and after 1 minute add the peas and mangetout/snow peas. Boil for a further 1 minute before draining, then transfer to a bowl of iced water to refresh. Drain all the peas and beans and put to one side.

For the dressing, put the olive oil and white wine vinegar in a large mixing bowl with a good pinch of salt, and beat with a fork to dissolve the salt in the vinegar. Add the mustard, crème fraîche and shallot and mix well again. Pop the mixed peas and beans and the new potatoes in the bowl with the dressing and mix well.

Just before serving, add the parsley, mint and ham hock to the dressed peas and beans and toss together. Season to taste with sea salt and ground black pepper, then sprinkle the pea shoots on top, to garnish, if using.

Asparagus & Salmon Frittata

I am a great believer in using fresh, seasonal produce and this is a wonderful dish for a May day, when asparagus comes into season. The crunchier the asparagus the better. You can find hot smoked salmon fillets in most supermarkets, or even your local deli. If you can't find them, a poached salmon fillet works just as well, or you could also try it with smoked trout for a different flavour combination.

Bring a pan of salted water to the boil and blanch the asparagus for about 1½–2 minutes, until just tender. Drain, then immediately plunge the asparagus into iced water to refresh. Drain again and leave to dry.

In a large mixing bowl, combine the eggs, cream cheese, lemon zest and juice, salt and black pepper. Stir in the salmon, most of the herbs, and the blanched asparagus.

Preheat a grill/broiler to high.

Heat a little olive oil in a frying pan set over a medium heat. Add the shallots and sauté until translucent, but do not brown. Pour the frittata mixture over the shallots and make sure the asparagus is evenly distributed and lying flat in the pan. Cook for about 4–5 minutes.

Drizzle a little olive oil over the top of the frittata, then transfer the frying pan to under the hot grill/broiler and cook for a further 4–5 minutes, until golden on top and puffed around the sides. Remove from the heat and allow to cool before running a spatula around the edge of the frittata and removing from the pan. Slice into wedges to serve.

200 g/7 oz. trimmed asparagus
6 large eggs
2 tablespoons cream cheese
finely grated zest and freshly
    squeezed juice of 1 lemon
150 g/5½ oz. hot smoked salmon,
    broken into bite-sized chunks
a handful of chopped fresh dill
    (or parsley, if you prefer)
2 shallots, diced
olive oil, for frying
sea salt and ground black pepper

a 23-cm/9-inch ovenproof frying pan

serves 6

Simply Dressed Green Salad

Sometimes less is more, and this is definitely the case with this little green number. It works beautifully as an accompaniment to the frittata and mozzarella tart. Actually, it works as an accompaniment with most things...

1 tablespoon olive oil
freshly squeezed juice of 1 lemon
1 bag rocket/arugula, washed
1 bag watercress, washed
1 fennel, head and leaves chopped
1 avocado, pitted and sliced

a bunch of fresh parsley, roughly
    chopped
sea salt and black pepper

serves 6

In a large salad bowl, whisk together the olive oil and lemon juice and season with salt and pepper.

Add the salad leaves and fennel to the bowl and toss to coat in the dressing. Finally, toss in the sliced avocado and chopped parsely before serving.

1 tablespoon olive oil

1 tablespoon balsamic vinegar

2–3 large beef/beefsteak tomatoes, thinly sliced

1 red onion, peeled and cut into wedges

a pinch of sugar

375 g/13 oz. ready-rolled puff pastry

200 g/7 oz. buffalo mozzarella, torn or sliced

a bunch of fresh basil, torn

sea salt and ground black pepper

serves 6

Buffalo Mozzarella, Beef Tomato & Basil Puff Tart

This is such a simple recipe to do, and takes minutes to make. You can experiment with all sorts of different toppings; goats' cheese works beautifully instead of mozzarella, use sun-blushed tomatoes instead of beef tomatoes, or try adding anchovies.

Preheat the oven to 220°C (425°F) Gas 7.

Put the olive oil and balsamic vinegar in a bowl, add the tomato slices and onion wedges and gently stir to coat in the dressing. Add a pinch of sugar and season with salt and pepper.

Trim the pastry into a 25–30-cm/10–12-inch rectangle and transfer to a baking sheet. Score a border around the pastry about 1 cm/½ inch from the edge, but do not cut all the way through.

Arrange the tomato and onion on the pastry in rows, with the tomato slightly overlapping, being careful not to go over the scored border, then scatter the torn mozzarella on top of the tomato and onion.

Bake in the preheated oven for 20–25 minutes or until the pastry is golden and the tomatoes are cooked right through and are bubbling hot.

Finish by sprinkling the fresh torn basil over the tart just before serving.

Strawberry Slush

Forget those additive-packed slushies whirling around in vats like toxic waste, this is a delicious cooling summer drink that kids will love and that hasn't a sniff of an e-preservative in sight. For adults, you could add a few shots of rum or tequila and serve as a strawberry daiquiri in cocktail glasses with sugar-frosted rims.

400 g/3 cups fresh strawberries, hulled

freshly squeezed juice of ½ lemon

1 teaspoon caster/superfine sugar

a few sprigs of fresh mint, plus extra sprigs to garnish

a handful of ice cubes, plus extra to serve

about 500 ml/2 cups softly sparkling water

serves 4–6

Put the strawberries in a blender with the lemon juice, sugar, mint and a handful of ice cubes. Pour in the sparkling water to just cover the ice and fruit and whizz in the blender for a minute or two.

Fill a jug/pitcher or a thermos with ice, then sieve/strain the blended cooler into the jug/pitcher or thermos to remove the strawberry seeds. Serve garnished with sprigs of fresh mint.

Rosewater Pavlova

The dessert that everyone loves. I have given a simple pavlova a twist by adding rosewater for a scented, perfumed quality, like a summer garden in bloom. You could also try flavouring creams and even meringues with lavender or orange-blossom water, too. If you can find candied rose petals (or have the time to make them yourself) sprinkle them over the top to garnish. If you are planning a picnic away from your garden, it is best to take the meringue, cream and raspberries in separate containers and assemble just before serving.

Preheat the oven to 120°C (250°F) Gas ½.

In a large mixing bowl, whisk the egg whites with an electric hand whisk until they just form stiff peaks. Gradually add the sugar, a couple of tablespoons at a time, whisking well between each addition. When all of the sugar is added, continue whisking for 3–4 minutes or until the meringue is stiff and glossy and stands up in peaks, then whisk in the cornflour/cornstarch and vinegar.

Spoon the mixture onto the prepared baking sheet and use a palette knife to shape it into a circle about 20-cm/8-inches in diameter. Bake in the preheated oven for 1½ hours, then turn the oven off, leave the door ajar and leave the meringue inside to cool completely (you could make the meringue the day before and leave to cool overnight).

When cool, carefully peel the meringue off the baking parchment and place on a serving dish. Don't worry too much if it breaks – there is plenty of topping to hide the cracks!

Put the cream in a mixing bowl and whisk until just thickening up. Add the rosewater and sugar and carry on whipping for a few more minutes until the cream is thick enough to spread. Spoon the rosewater cream onto the meringue, heap the fresh raspberries on top and dust with icing/confectioners' sugar.

For the meringue:
4 egg whites
225 g/1¼ cups golden caster/natural
    superfine sugar
1 teaspoon cornflour/cornstarch
1 teaspoon white wine vinegar

For the topping:
250 ml/1 cup double/heavy cream
1 tablespoon rosewater
1 tablespoon caster/superfine sugar
350 g/2 cups fresh raspberries
icing/confectioners' sugar, for dusting

a baking sheet lined with non-stick
    baking parchment

serves 6

6 large eggs, separated
200 g/1 cup caster/superfine sugar
250 g/1 cup mascarpone cheese
250 ml/1 cup double/heavy cream
300 ml/1¼ cups strong black coffee
200 ml/¾ cup brandy
50–60 bite-sized amaretti biscuits/
   cookies (amarettino, or 25–30
   sponge fingers/ladyfingers, if
   you prefer)
shaved chocolate, to decorate
cocoa powder, for dusting

6 jam or kilner jars, with lids

serves 6

Potted Amaretti Tiramisù

Not only does this dessert look great served in individual lidded jam or kilner jars, which adds a novelty factor, but potting the tiramisù also allows for easy-peasy transportation. Make sure you pack the jars in a very well insulated cool bag with plenty of ice packs so they remain cool. In this recipe I use amaretti biscuits/cookies as they add a depth of flavour; the taste of almond works beautifully with coffee, cream and chocolate.

In a large mixing bowl and using an electric hand whisk, beat the eggs yolks with the sugar until thick and creamy. In a separate bowl, beat the egg whites to stiff peaks and set aside.

Add the mascarpone to the egg yolk mixture a spoonful at a time, whisking well between each addition, until smooth. Whisk the cream to soft peaks, then fold into the mascarpone and yolk mixture with a metal spoon. Finally, fold the egg whites into the mixture.

Combine the coffee with the brandy in a bowl. Dip half the amaretti biscuits/cookies in the liquid, soaking completely, then use them to line the bottom of the jars. Spoon half of the mascarpone mixture over the amaretti bases, dividing it equally between the 6 jars.

Dip the remaining biscuits/cookies in the coffee and brandy and arrange on top of the mascarpone in all 6 jars to create a layered effect, then spoon over the remaining mascarpone mixture. Pop the lids on the jars and chill for about 2 hours. Sprinkle with shaved chocolate and dust generously with cocoa powder before serving or packing in a very well insulated cool bag to take with you.

2 Bohemian Picnic

The heady night bazaars of North Africa and the Middle East have inspired this picnic. Mezze, a traditional way of eating in the Middle East, is a collection of sharing plates, rather like tapas, that everyone can dive into and which are ideal for a picnic. To create the scene, hang Moroccan lanterns or patterned sari fabric from trees or dot them around a ground rug – a Persian-style one if you have it, or a large coloured tablecloth works just as well. Indian bunting looks very pretty, as do large cushions or poufs to recline on. Beautiful earthenware pots and tagines make effective serving bowls for the delicious feast, and serve mint tea in pretty coloured tea glasses resting on a silver tray.

Mezze Platter of Baba Ghanoush with Flatbreads

Rack of Lamb Stuffed with Feta & Mint

Spiced Citrus Couscous

Wild Rocket, Pomegranate & Squash Salad with a Balsamic Dressing

Grilled Halloumi Cheese & Mediterranean Vegetable Stack

Caramelized Figs with Saffron Honey & Vanilla Mascarpone

Pear & Almond Tart

Mint Tea Cocktail

Mezze Platter of Baba Ghanoush with Flatbreads

Baba ghanoush is a gorgeous alternative to hoummus. The trick to making a cracking baba ghanoush is by roasting the aubergines/eggplant until the skin is blackened, which will give this dish a rich, heady smokiness. You can serve it with raw vegetable crudités as well as flatbreads, if you wish.

Baba Ghanoush

Preheat the oven to 200°C (400°F) Gas 6.

Put the whole aubergines/eggplants on the prepared baking sheet, side by side and roast in the preheated oven for about 30 minutes, or until the skins are blistered and blackened. Remove the aubergines/eggplants from the oven and leave to cool.

Once cool, scrape all the flesh from the aubergines/eggplants into a mixing bowl, discarding the charred skins. Add the crushed garlic, most of the lemon juice (a little flesh of the lemon is also quite nice), the tahini and 2 tablespoons of the olive oil. Using a fork, mash up the flesh as much as you can until everything is well incorporated into a chunky purée. Season with a pinch of salt and pepper and taste. It should be smoky, sweet, garlicky, tangy. If the paste is too thick or the taste of garlic is too pungent, add a little more lemon juice and olive oil. Set the baba ghanoush aside while you make the flatbreads.

When you are ready to serve, sprinkle your chosen garnish on top to add colour and flavour, drizzle with a little olive oil and serve with the flatbreads.

4 aubergines/eggplants
2 garlic cloves, crushed
freshly squeezed juice of 1 lemon
1 generous tablespoon tahini paste
2–3 tablespoons olive oil
sea salt and ground black pepper
a sprinkling of pomegranate seeds, chopped fresh coriander/cilantro, ½ teaspoon toasted cumin seeds, or a teaspoon of harissa paste, to garnish

a baking sheet, greased with olive oil

Flatbreads

In a jug/pitcher dissolve the yeast in the warm water and leave for 10 minutes.

Sift the flour into a large mixing bowl and make a well in the middle. Add the yogurt and mix well. Now gently pour a little of the water and yeast mixture into the well in the flour, along with a good glug of the olive oil. Knead the dough with your hands to combine, bringing the flour into the middle of the bowl and adding a little more of the yeast mixture and the olive oil at a time. When all the ingredients are combined, bring the dough out of the bowl and knead it on a floured surface for about 10 minutes until it is shiny and smooth. Place the dough back in the bowl, cover with a clean tea/dish towel and leave in a warm, dry place (an airing cupboard is ideal) for 1½–2 hours, until almost doubled in size.

When the dough has proved, give it a final knead to dispel any air, then divide the mixture into 6 balls. On a floured surface, roll out each ball to approximately ½ cm/¼ inch thick and sprinkle with sea salt.

Here, you can either preheat your oven to 200°C (400°F) Gas 6, put the flatbreads on the prepared baking sheet and bake for 6–8 minutes; or brush the breads with olive oil on both sides and place on a smoking hot griddle pan for around 1–2 minutes on each side, until golden. Serve on a platter with the Baba Ghanoush.

½ teaspoon dried/active dry yeast
250 ml/1 cup warm water
500 g/4 cups plain/all-purpose or wholemeal/whole-wheat flour, plus extra for dusting
400 g/1⅔ cups plain yogurt
40 ml/3 tablespoons olive oil (plus extra for brushing the flatbreads, if cooking on a griddle)
sea salt

a baking sheet, lightly greased, or a griddle pan

serves 6

200 g/7 oz. feta cheese

2 tablespoons finely chopped fresh mint

2 tablespoons finely chopped fresh flatleaf parsley

freshly squeezed juice and grated zest of 1 lemon

2 lamb racks (7–8 cutlets on each rack), fat trimmed away to expose the bone at each end

3 tablespoons olive oil

sea salt and ground black pepper

toasted pine nuts, to garnish

unwaxed kitchen twine
a large baking pan, greased

serves 6

Rack of Lamb Stuffed with Feta & Mint

Lamb is the staple meat in the Middle East, besides camel! This dish takes influences from Persia and chucks a hint of Mediterranean in the mix, too. The lamb works just beautifully as a main meal with the spiced couscous.

Preheat the oven to 200°C (400°F) Gas 6.

Put the feta cheese in a mixing bowl and use a fork to mash it until almost smooth. Add the mint, parsley and lemon juice and zest, and stir until combined.

Use a knife to cut down the length of each lamb rack, close to the bones, about 3 cm/1¼ inches deep, to create a cavity for the stuffing. Divide the feta into 2 and stuff each lamb rack with the mixture. Tie some kitchen twine around every other cutlet to keep the rack together, then place the racks in the prepared baking pan, side by side so they remain upright. Drizzle over the olive oil and season well with salt and pepper. Bake in the preheated oven for 25–30 minutes for medium, or leave 10 minutes longer if you prefer your lamb well done.

Garnish with the toasted pine nuts and serve with the couscous and squash salad (see page 30). If you wish, you can slice the lamb into cutlets before packing into a cool bag to make it easier to transport.

250 g/1⅔ cups couscous

250 ml/1 cup boiling water

100 g/⅔ cup very finely chopped dried, ready-to-eat apricots

a handful of raisins

½ teaspoon ground turmeric

½ teaspoon ground coriander

½ teaspoon ground cumin

a small handful of fresh coriander/cilantro, chopped finely

a small handful of fresh mint, chopped finely

2–3 tablespoons olive oil, or to taste

freshly squeezed juice and grated zest of 1 lemon

freshly squeezed juice and grated zest of 1 orange

85 g/¾ cup flaked/slivered almonds

For the crispy onion garnish:

175 ml/¾ cup sunflower oil, for frying

1 onion

1 tablespoon plain/all-purpose flour

sea salt and ground black pepper

serves 6

Spiced Citrus Couscous

Citrusy, fruity and spicy, this couscous dish is heaven sent. It's great to see couscous as such a popular accompaniment these days, and it's no wonder. Couscous is easy to prepare, nutritious and yummy to boot. If you want to try a simpler couscous dish, try tabbouleh. Simply mix the soaked couscous with handfuls of chopped parsley and mint, chopped tomatoes, cubes of feta cheese and red onion.

First, make the crispy onion garnish. Pour the sunflower oil into a shallow frying pan set over a high heat.

Slice the onion in half, then slice each half into half moons as thinly as you can. Put the flour on a plate and season with salt and pepper, then toss the onion slices in the flour to coat generously.

By now the oil should be smoking hot, so, in small batches, fry off the onions until golden brown and really crispy. Remove the onion from the hot pan with a slotted spoon and transfer to a plate lined with paper towels to blot out any excess oil and leave to cool.

Put the couscous in a shallow bowl and pour over the boiling water. Cover the bowl with clingfilm/plastic wrap and leave for 5–10 minutes, until the couscous has absorbed all the water and puffed up. Mix well with a fork to separate any grains, then stir in the dried fruit, spices and herbs and mix really well.

In a separate small bowl, combine the olive oil with the juice and zest of the lemon and orange a beat well. Taste this and add more oil if it is too tart.

Gently pour the dressing over the couscous and mix well. Lastly, just before serving, scatter over the crispy onions and flaked/slivered almonds, to garnish.

To persuade a friend to stay for lunch is a triumph and a precious honour. To entertain many together is to honour them all mutually. It is equally an honour to be a guest.

Claudia Roden

1 large butternut squash
a drizzle of olive oil
1 tablespoon crushed dried chilli/hot
    pepper flakes (optional)
2 tablespoons coriander seeds
2 tablespoons cumin seeds
sea salt and ground black pepper
200 g/7 oz. rocket/arugula leaves,
    washed and dried
seeds from 1 large pomegranate
    (save the juice) or 150 g/5½ oz.
    pre-packed pomegranate seeds
a handful of fresh mint leaves,
    stalks removed

For the balsamic dressing:
2 tablespoons balsamic vinegar
freshly squeezed juice of ½ lemon
1 tablespoon pomegranate molasses
    (or leftover pomegranate juice if
    you cannot find)
3 tablespoons olive oil
sea salt and ground black pepper

serves 6

Wild Rocket, Pomegranate & Squash Salad with a Balsamic Dressing

Simple ingredients that pack a punch with flavour, that is what this salad is all about. A great one for vegetarians, too. I like to use butternut squash as its sweetness works well with the heat from the chilli and spices, but pumpkin or roasted sweet potatoes also work well. You can buy pre-packed pomegranate seeds from many supermarkets in the fruit and vegetable aisle, but if you have to extract them from the fruit yourself, the juice that runs out makes a lovely addition to the dressing.

Preheat the oven to 200°C (400°F) Gas 6.
Slice the butternut squash in half lengthways and discard all the seeds and stringy bits (leave the skin on). Slice the halves into long strips about 8 mm/ ⅜ inch thick. Arrange these on a baking sheet.
In a pestle and mortar, roughly grind the chilli/hot pepper flakes and spice seeds together, then sprinkle them evenly over the butternut squash. Drizzle a really good glug of olive oil over and season well with salt and pepper. Pop in the preheated oven and roast for about 25–30 minutes, until the edges are just browning and the squash is squishy and cooked but not dried out. Leave to cool.
Toss the rocket/arugula leaves, pomegranate seeds and mint leaves together. Transfer to a transportable container and arrange the squash on top.
To make the balsamic dressing, combine all the ingredients together in a jar and shake well to mix. Pack into the cool bag and drizzle over the salad just before serving.

Grilled Halloumi Cheese & Mediterranean Vegetable Stack

Roasted vegetables and halloumi are a wonderful amalgamation of tastes and textures, but be careful not to overcook the halloumi as this can make it a tad rubbery and squeaky, but still delicious though.

Preheat the oven to 220°C (425°F) Gas 7.

Slice the aubergine/eggplant and the courgettes/zucchini widthways into 1-cm/½-inch thick slices. Peel and chop the onion into ⅛ th wedges. Lastly, chop the peppers in half, remove the seeds and cut into 1 cm/½ inch thick strips. Drizzle a little olive oil on a baking sheet and arrange the vegetables with the rosemary sprigs on top. Drizzle over more olive oil, making sure there is plenty on the aubergine/eggplant slices as they tend to dry out in the oven, and season very well with salt and pepper. Roast in the preheated oven for 30–40 minutes, until the vegetables are tender and lightly browned on the outside. Leave to cool before squeezing the lemon juice lightly over all of the vegetables.

Brush a griddle pan with olive oil and set over a medium–high heat. Cut the halloumi lengthways into around 6 slices per block and cook on the griddle for 30 seconds on each side until lightly golden lines appear.

To assemble, start with a slice of the halloumi cheese on the bottom and layer up your vegetables and 1 further slice of halloumi per stack. Secure with cocktail sticks/toothpicks to keep the stacks together whilst transporting, but remember to remove them before serving!

1 large aubergine/eggplant
3 small courgettes/zucchini, any colour
1 large red onion
2 red bell peppers
3–4 tablespoons olive oil
3 large sprigs of rosemary
freshly squeezed juice of ½ lemon
2 x 250 g/9 oz. blocks of halloumi cheese, sliced
sea salt and ground black pepper

a griddle pan
cocktail sticks/toothpicks

serves 6

6 ripe figs, washed and patted dry

For the vanilla mascarpone:
500 g/2 cups mascarpone cheese
seeds from 2 vanilla pods/beans
1 tablespoon icing/confectioners'
   sugar, plus extra for dusting

For the saffron honey syrup:
200 g/1 cup caster/granulated sugar
3 tablespoons honey
¼ teaspoon saffron threads
1 cinnamon stick
1 star anise
1 clove

serves 6

Caramelized Figs with Saffron Honey & Vanilla Mascarpone

Figs – a food of the gods! When you get a truly ripe fig the taste can be sensational. I almost loath to adulterise a ripe fig, so if you manage to get your hands on some in season then you could just slice them and serve fresh with the vanilla mascarpone. This recipe caramelizes the beauties with subtle saffron and sweet honey, two popular ingredients in the Middle East. The flavours are a combustion of wonder and the perfect finale to your bohemian feast.

Start by making the saffron honey syrup. Put the sugar, honey, saffron, cinnamon stick, star anise and clove in a saucepan along with 200 ml/¾ cup water and bring gently to the boil over a low heat. Simmer for at least 15 minutes, until the syrup has reduced to a quarter of the original volume, then remove from the heat and allow to cool.

In a small mixing bowl, fold together the mascarpone, vanilla seeds and the icing/confectioners' sugar until well combined. Transfer to a transportable container and keep cool until ready to serve.

Preheat the grill/broiler. Cut a deep cross shape in the top of the figs and place them on a baking sheet. Dust with icing/confectioners' sugar before placing them under the grill/broiler for about 5 minutes, until the sugar is bubbling and turning golden. Remove from the heat and allow them to cool before transferring them to a plastic container. Pour the cooled syrup over the figs, pop the lid on and allow them to infuse while you find your picnic spot! To serve, place a fig on a plate or in a bowl, add a dollop of the sweet mascarpone and drizzle some of that delicious syrup over the top.

3 ripe pears
150 g/¾ cup caster/granulated sugar
freshly squeezed juice of 1 lime
375 g/12 oz. ready-made sweet
    shortcrust pastry
plain/all-purpose flour, for dusting
crème fraîche, to serve (optional)

For the filling:
75 g/5 tablespoons butter, softened
75 g/⅓ cup light brown muscovado
    sugar
100 g/1 cup ground almonds
50 g/6 tablespoons self-raising flour
1 tablespoon pear schnapps or
    calvados
2 eggs, beaten
4 tablespoons apple sauce, plus
    a little extra to glaze

a deep 25-cm/10-inch fluted tart pan
an apple corer

serves 6

Pear & Almond Tart

This tart is easy to transport and can be made the day before and kept in the fridge. Serve a slice just on its own or with a dollop of crème fraîche on the side.

Peel the skin from the pears and core but leave whole. Put the pears in a large saucepan with the sugar and lime juice, cover with water, then bring to the boil. Turn the heat down and simmer very gently for 10 minutes, then remove the pears from the pan and leave to cool (you can discard the poaching liquid).

Preheat the oven to 180°C (350°F) Gas 4.

On a floured surface, roll out the pastry to 3 mm/⅛ inch thick and use it to line the tart pan. Cut off any excess pastry, then chill for 30 minutes. Once chilled, use a fork to prick the pastry all over, line with baking parchment, fill the pan with baking beans and bake in the preheated oven for 15 minutes. Remove the beans and parchment paper and leave to cool. Leave the oven on.

Meanwhile, make the almond filling by combining the butter, sugar, almonds, flour, scnapps and eggs in a large mixing bowl and beating until smooth and creamy. (You could also do this in a food processor if you have one.)

Using a palette knife, spread the apple sauce over the base of the pastry, then gently pour over the almond mixture. Halve the poached pears, then slice and fan them out before arranging them on top of the tart. Pop the tart back in the oven for about 40 minutes, until golden brown and the almond filling is set.

Once you remove the tart from the oven, brush a little more apple sauce over the top to give a gorgeous shiny glaze. Leave to cool before serving.

Mint Tea Cocktail

You cannot talk Middle Eastern cuisine without including mint tea in the equation. In Morocco especially, mint tea is synonymous with hospitality; usually this is handfuls of fresh mint and enough sugar to keep the spoon vertical, covered with boiling water. This cocktail chills the mint tea, throws in a touch of gin and has much less sugar than the tea you might find on the streets of Marrakech.

In a large saucepan, bring 1 litre/quart of water to the boil. Once bubbling, remove from the heat and add the peppermint tea bags and a good handful of mint leaves to the pan. Allow to steep for approximately 3–5 minutes before fishing out the tea bags and mint. Add the sugar and stir to dissolve, allow to cool before decanting into a jug/pitcher and putting in the refrigerator to chill.

Once thoroughly chilled, decant the cocktail into a thermos flask filled with ice along with the gin, if using. To serve, pour the chilled cocktail into glasses and garnish with lemon and lime slices and mint leaves.

4 peppermint tea bags
a handful of fresh mint leaves, plus
extra to garnish
2 tablespoons caster/granulated
sugar
200 ml/¾ cup gin (optional)
4 handfuls of ice cubes
½ lime, whole sliced
½ lemon, whole sliced

serves 6

3 Bike Ride Picnic

There is nothing like feeling the wind in your hair and the warm sun on your skin on a meandering bike ride. Of course, you need to have a pit-stop now and again to refuel and this menu offers delicious treats, full of energy, that can keep you peddling all day. When planning a bike ride picnic, you must be aware that limited space does not always allow you to pack a huge hamper of goodies. You need to think savvy and prepare delicious bites that can fit into a back-pack, pannier or bike basket. The dishes below are all about eating on the go, and not necessarily needing all the utensils under the sun – plates, knives and forks, napkins, etc. – to enjoy the food. Simply find a shady spot under the boughs of a tree, park up the bikes, stretch out your legs, sip cool peach iced tea and indulge in a feast.

Goats' Cheese, Thyme & Red Onion Tartlets

Salad Jars

Sweet Potato Falafel with Homemade Toum

Hand-risen Pork Pies

Squidgy Date Cake

Peach Iced Tea

Goats' Cheese, Thyme & Red Onion Tartlets

Caramelized red onion and goats' cheese are one of those flavour marriages made in heaven. Add rich golden pastry and fragrant thyme to the mix and you have a delicious tart, scrummy to eat at home with a baby leaf salad, or on the go whilst tackling a 30 degree incline on two wheels.

To make the pastry, put the thyme leaves, flour, butter and lard in a food processor and mix on the pulse setting until you have a breadcrumb consistency. Gradually add about 2–3 tablespoons of water to form a soft dough. You now have a lovely thyme pastry. Remove from the food processor, wrap in clingfilm/plastic wrap and leave it in the fridge to chill for about 30 minutes.

While you are waiting for the pastry to chill, you can prepare the caramelized onions. Pop the red onions, butter, sugar, balsamic vinegar, cassis and seasoning into a large frying pan and cook over a very low heat. Watch carefully as the caramelizing process starts and the liquid starts to thicken and bubble, as it may burn. Stir the onions occasionally to prevent clumping. Continue to simmer until nearly all of the liquid has evaporated and it is a sticky jam-like consistency.

Now preheat the oven to 200°C (400°F) Gas 6 and place a large baking sheet in there to heat up.

Take your pastry out of the fridge and divide it into 6 equal portions. On a floured surface, roll out a portion to a circle 5 mm/¼ inch thick and use it to line one of the prepared tartlet pans, trimming away the excess pastry around the edge. Repeat to line all 6 tartlet pans, then line the pastry with baking parchment and baking beans. Place the tartlet pans on the hot baking sheet and bake in the preheated oven for about 10 minutes. Remove the beans and lining paper and return to the oven for 5 minutes, then leave the pastry crusts to cool for a few minutes in the pans. Leave the oven on.

Divide the caramelized red onion jam between the tartlets and place a slice of goats' cheese on top, followed by a twist of salt and pepper and a sprig of thyme for decoration. Return to the oven for about 10–15 minutes, or until the top of the goats' cheese is bubbling and tinged with brown. Leave the tartlets to cool before packing into airtight boxes and loading onto your bike.

6 thick slices from a log of Chèvre goats' cheese
6 sprigs of fresh thyme

For the pastry:
3 small sprigs of fresh thyme, stalks removed
160 g/1¼ cups plain/all-purpose flour, plus extra for dusting
40 g/3 tablespoons butter
40 g/3½ tablespoons lard

For the caramelized onions:
3 large red onions, finely sliced
55 g/4 tablespoons butter
40 g/3 tablespoons soft brown sugar
2 tablespoons balsamic vinegar
3 tablespoons cassis liqueur
sea salt and ground black pepper

6 x 10-cm/4-inch loose-based tartlet pans, greased

serves 6

Life is like riding a bicycle – in order to keep your balance, you must keep moving.

Albert Einstein

2 large beef/beefsteak tomatoes
2 tablespoons olive oil
freshly squeezed juice of ½ lemon
5 carrots
500 g/1 lb. raw beets
2 large oranges
1 recipe Cucumber, Pineapple & Dill
   Salad (see opposite)
1 recipe Herby Citrus Quinoa
   (see opposite)
90 g/3 oz. rocket/arugula leaves
2 tablespoons sunflower seeds
sea salt and ground black pepper

6 Kilner jars

serves 6

Salad Jars

This recipe is about bringing a few different components together and, as you layer up the different elements, the different flavours compliment each other. You can vary this recipe and bring in salad ideas of your own, too. I often like to add the flageolet bean salad (see page 13) or a three-bean salad, couscous or tabbouleh (see page 28) would also work well. If you are heading out on a bike ride, you need your picnic to be quite compact, the elements of your meal being able to fit in a back-pack, pannier or small bike basket. Salad jars work wonders for this and the kaleidoscope of colours looks very inviting. Use large, lidded jars and don't forget the forks to eat it with.

To start, slice the beef tomatoes into 1 cm/½ inch-thick slices. Discard the top and tail ends so you have even slices. Lay the slices flat on a large dish, sprinkle generously with salt and pepper and drizzle with olive oil and a squeeze of lemon juice. Leave to one side at room temperature until needed.

Grate the carrots and then, separately, the beets. Put these, again, to one side. Lastly, peel and segment the oranges.

You are now ready to build your jars. Start with the beets as the purple does tend to stain the other components. Spoon 2–3 tablespoons grated beets into the bottom of each jar, then lay about 3 segments of orange over the top.

Next comes the Cucumber, Pineapple & Dill Salad. Spoon in 2–3 tablespoons and gently press it down so it evens out. Place a slice of tomato into the jar, reserving the oil and lemon dressing from the tomato plate to use later. You should be able to start seeing the layers come together.

I would go for 4–5 tablespoons of the Herby Citrus Quinoa next, followed by 2–3 tablespoons of grated carrot, then a good handful of rocket/arugula leaves and a sprinkling of sunflower seeds on top. Finally, drizzle with the remaining olive oil and lemon dressing, seal the jar lids and you're ready to go.

Cucumber, Pineapple & Dill Salad

Top and tail the cucumber and peel if it is thick skinned. Now chop it lengthways and then lengthways again so it is quartered. Dice down the cucumber strips in 1-cm/½-inch rows until it is cut into small pieces, then transfer them to a mixing bowl, along with the drained pineapple chunks and mix together.

Roughly chop the dill leaves, discarding any tough stalks, and sprinkle over the salad. Season lightly with salt and pepper and give it a final mix so all the ingredients are well combined.

1 cucumber
1 x 432 g/15 oz. can pineapple
    chunks in natural juice, drained
6 sprigs of fresh dill
sea salt and ground black pepper

serves 6

Herby Citrus Quinoa

First, fill your kettle with water and start to boil.

Rinse the quinoa in a sieve/strainer under cold running water, then transfer to a saucepan. Cover the quinoa with the boiling water until it is just covered and set the saucepan over a medium heat. Cook for about 15–20 minutes, until the grains are tender, then drain well and leave to cool in a mixing bowl.

Using the leaves of the herbs only, put the herbs, garlic and capers into a food processor and chop on a pulse setting, but make sure you don't purée the mixture. Add the lemon juice and olive oil and season with salt and pepper and pulse once or twice more until everything is combined.

Now crumble the feta cheese over the cooled quinoa, pour over the herby dressing and mix well.

300 g/1½ cups quinoa
a handful of fresh basil, very finely
    chopped
a handful of fresh flatleaf parsley,
    very finely chopped
a small handful of fresh mint, very
    finely chopped
2 garlic cloves, crushed
150 g/5½ oz. feta cheese, crumbled
freshly squeezed juice of 1 lemon
2 tablespoons olive oil
1 tablespoon capers, drained
sea salt and ground black pepper

serves 6

3 medium sweet potatoes

1 x 410-g/14-oz. can chickpeas, drained and rinsed

180 g/1¼ cups gram (chickpea) flour

1 banana shallot, or 2 regular shallots, finely diced

3 garlic cloves, crushed

1½ teaspoons ground cumin

2 teaspoons ground coriander

3 handfuls of fresh coriander/cilantro, finely chopped

freshly squeezed juice of 1 lemon

sea salt and ground black pepper

a sprinkling of sesame seeds (optional)

To serve:

6 whole pitta breads

2 tablespoons hoummus, or to taste

½ green cabbage, raw, shredded

3 tomatoes, sliced

3 baby gem/Bibb lettuces, leaves

6 tablespoons Toum Garlic Sauce

a baking sheet, lined and greased

serves 6

Sweet Potato Falafel with Homemade Toum

These falafel pitta pockets hail from Lebanese cooking. The sweet potatoes add a lovely dimension to the traditional falafel mix and Toum sauce, as it is known in the Middle East, is an absolute must. You can buy falafels from any good deli or supermarket but it's fun to make your own and they always taste miles better home-cooked.

Preheat the oven to 200°C (400°F) Gas 6.

Roast the sweet potatoes in their skins for about 1 hour until cooked through. (Alternatively, you can microwave the sweet potatoes, whole, for 15–20 minutes until tender.) Leave the potatoes until cool enough to handle, peel off and discard the skin, then chop roughly.

Put the cooked potatoes, chickpeas, gram flour, shallot, garlic, cumin, ground coriander, fresh coriander/cilantro and lemon juice into a large mixing bowl. Season well with salt and pepper, then mash with a fork or potato masher until smooth. (You can also do this in a food processor if you have one.) The mixture should be sticky to touch but not wet. If the mixture is still quite sloppy you could add a little more gram flour.

Using a dessertspoon, scoop spoonfuls of the mix and shape into 18 balls, about the size of a ping-pong ball. Arrange the balls a little way apart on the prepared baking sheet, then flatten each into a patty. Pop the baking sheet in the fridge for 1 hour, or in the freezer for 20 minutes if you are pushed for time.

When the patties are chilled, sprinkle over the sesame seeds, if using, pop them in the oven and bake at 200°C (400°F) Gas 6 for 15 minutes until lovely and brown all over.

To serve, toast the pittas, then split them open. Spread a thin layer of hoummus on the inside before stuffing with cabbage, tomatoes, lettuce and 3 of the falafels. Top with lashings of garlicky Toum sauce just before serving.

Toum Garlic Sauce

245 g/1 cup Greek-style yogurt

2 tablespoons mayonnaise

½ tablespoon extra virgin olive oil

2 sprigs of mint, stalks removed and leaves very finely chopped

2 garlic cloves, crushed

a squeeze of lemon juice

a pinch of sea salt

serves 6

In a mixing bowl, whisk the yogurt and mayonnaise together until smooth and creamy. Whilst whisking, slowly pour in the olive oil. Finally, add the chopped mint, crushed garlic, a squeeze of lemon juice and a pinch of sea salt and give it a final mix until everything is well combined.

For the filling:

400 g/14 oz. boneless pork shoulder

110 g/4 oz. bacon lardons/very
    thickly sliced bacon, cut into cubes

2 sprigs of thyme, leaves only, finely
    chopped

1 sprig of sage, leaves only, finely
    chopped

½ teaspoon anchovy sauce
    (such as Geo Watkins)

a pinch of ground nutmeg

½ teaspoon ground mace

sea salt and ground black pepper

For the pastry:

340 g/2⅔ cups strong plain bread
    flour, plus extra for dusting

a good pinch of salt

40 ml/3 tablespoons milk

120 g/½ cup lard, cubed

1 large egg yolk, beaten, to glaze

For the jelly:

1 pig's trotter

1 bouquet garni

1 carrot

1 celery stalk

5 sheets of leaf gelatine/1 envelope
    powdered gelatin

Branston pickle, to serve

a jam jar, roughly 7-cm/2¾-inch diameter,
    or a pie dolly

an 8-cm/3¼-inch round pastry cutter

a kitchen funnel

serves 6

Hand-risen Pork Pies

All hail the traditional British pork pie! The flaky pastry and meaty filling, along with that delicious flavoured jelly, is one of things that makes Britain great. Making your own pork pies is as easy as 1-2-3, although do try to allow yourself 2 days, what with all the marinating and solidifying that needs to take place to make a corking pork pie.

Firstly, chop the pork shoulder into coarse (about 5-mm/¼-inch) chunks. Put them in a large mixing bowl with all the other filling ingredients and mix well. Leave this in the fridge overnight to let all the lovely flavours combine.

For the pastry, sift the flour into a large mixing bowl and add the salt. Gently heat the milk and 50 ml/3½ tablespoons water in a saucepan and add the cubes of lard. When the lard has melted, increase the heat and bring to the boil. Take off the heat as the first bubbles appear and slowly pour over the flour, mixing everything together with a wooden spoon until it forms a firm dough.

Knead the dough on a lightly floured surface for around 5–8 minutes, then remove one third (which will be used to make the pie lids). The remaining dough should be cut into 6 equal portions and shaped into patties. Wrap all the pastry in clingfilm/plastic wrap and chill in the fridge overnight.

When you come to make the pies, preheat the oven to 220°C (425°F) Gas 7.

Cover the jam jar in clingfilm/plastic wrap and gently push the jar down into one of the dough patties – this should raise the dough up and around the jar. Gently mould the pastry up the sides to about 4 cm/1½ inches high. (You could also use a pie dolly for this.) Use the cling film/plastic wrap to help you gently remove the jar from the pastry cup. Follow this method with the remaining pieces of dough to make 6 pastry cups, then divide the filling mixture evenly between them.

On a floured surface, roll out the pastry reserved for the lids to about 5 mm/¼ inch thick and cut out 6 rounds using the pastry cutter. Using a pastry brush, paint some egg yolk around the top of the pastry cups and on the inside of a lid and gently press the lid down onto the pies. Use your finger and thumb to gently crimp the sides of the wall and lid together all the way around, making sure the pastry is sealed completely or the pie may collapse in the oven. Give each pie an egg wash (not the crimp though), then make a hole in the centre of the lid for the steam to escape and to be able to pour the jelly in later when the pies are cooked.

Place the pies on a baking sheet and bake in the preheated oven for about 1¼ hours until a rich, deep golden brown. Leave to cool on a wire rack.

For the jelly, put the pig's trotter, bouquet garni, carrot and celery stalk in a large saucepan with 5 litres/quarts of water and bring to the boil, then simmer for about 4 hours. Allow the water to evaporate down to about 500 ml/2 cups, but do not let the pan boil dry – top it up with more water if necessary. After 4 hours, strain the liquid stock into a measuring jug/cup – you will need 500 ml/2 cups. Dissolve the gelatine in the warm stock, continuously stirring until it thickens. It is now ready to fill the pies.

Insert a funnel into the hole in the lid of one of the pies (you may have to re-open this with a skewer) and slowly pour the jelly mixture into the hole until it just overflows. Repeat with the remaining 5 pies, then leave them, preferably overnight, to cool in a fridge. Eat cold with a teaspoon of Branston pickle. Yum!

Squidgy Date Cake

This gorgeously gooey cake is a delight to make and a even more of a delight to eat. The sticky sourness of the fruit is offset by the sweet rich dulce de leche. It only needs a sprinkling of sugar on top but is a perfect energy booster packed with all that dried fruit.

Preheat the oven to 190°C (375°F) Gas 5.

Pop the raisins, dates and currants in a saucepan together with the butter, dulce de leche and 275 ml/1 cup plus 2 tablespoons water. Slowly bring to the boil, stirring frequently to prevent the mixture from burning. Turn off the heat as soon as the first bubbles appear and leave to cool, but make sure you stir it a few times as it does so.

In a large mixing bowl, sift together the flours, bicarbonate of soda/baking soda and salt.

When the fruit mixture has cooled, fold it into the flour, along with the marmalade, until smooth and well combined. Transfer the batter to the prepared cake pan and sprinkle over a generous helping of sugar.

Put the cake in the middle of the preheated oven and bake for 1½ hours. (After 30 minutes, you may want to cover the cake with a sheet of baking parchment or kitchen foil to prevent the top over-browning.) Check the cake is springy to touch and a skewer inserted into the middle comes out clean. If not, bake for a further 15 minutes or so, depending on your oven, then test again.

Allow the cake to cool for 10 minutes before turning out of the pan. Set on a wire rack to cool completely, then cut into wedges and wrap in paper napkins to enjoy as a pit stop snack on your bicycle tour.

275 g/1¾ cups raisins
225 g/1½ cups pitted, chopped dates
120 g/1 scant cup dried (zante) currants
275 g/2 sticks plus 2 tablespoons butter
660 g/22 oz. dulce de leche
150 g/1 cup plus 2 tablespoons wholemeal/whole-wheat flour
150 g/1 cup plus 2 tablespoons plain/all-purpose flour
a pinch of salt
1 teaspoon bicarbonate of soda/baking soda
2 tablespoons marmalade
2 tablespoons unrefined granulated brown/raw cane sugar

a 23-cm/9-inch round deep loose-based cake pan, greased and double-lined with baking parchment

serves 6–8

Peach Iced Tea

There is something rather nostalgic about peach iced tea. It conjures up images of 1950s America; I wonder if Doris Day drank peach iced tea every day? This recipe adds a little bite of ginger and mint to compliment the peachy tea flavours.

1 tablespoon China or Darjeeling leaf tea
1 lemon, sliced
a 5-cm/2-inch piece of ginger, peeled and smashed
1 litre/quart boiling water

4–6 handfuls of ice cubes
6 peaches, peeled, pitted and diced
65 g/⅓ cup caster/superfine sugar
a few sprigs of mint, to garnish

serves 4–6

Put the tea leaves, lemon and ginger in a heatproof bowl and add the boiling water. Let the tea steep for 7–8 minutes.

Put 2 handfuls of ice into another bowl, strain over the tea and allow to cool.

In a blender, pulse the remaining ice, the peaches and the sugar until smooth, then pour in the cooled tea. Transfer the peach iced tea to the thermos flask to keep cool during your bike ride and serve garnished with a few sprigs of mint.

Choosing Your Menu

The list is endless as to what theme you can choose for your perfect picnic. From easy-to-pack food on the go, to more sophisticated dishes for a special gathering of friends and family, there are various things to consider – from the time of year and location of the picnic to the number of people and how much time you have to spend on preparing the food.

When planning, start by thinking of the occasion and the guests, as this will affect which theme you choose. Have you adults or kids or both attending? The finger food featured in the Teddy Bears' Picnic is perfect for little ones and would make a fabulous children's birthday party – they will love the mini Scotch Quails' Eggs and their dessert served in plant pots.

The gourmet dishes in the Luxe Picnic are definitely more for adult tastes and would work amazingly for an informal wedding or even a black-tie do, while the relaxed, family favourites featured in the Vintage Garden Party are perfect for a larger but still fuss-free gathering. Just remember, neither of these menus are particularly suited to less accessible locations, but are great if you are eating within reach of a kitchen or a car with plenty of boot/trunk space.

Consider also the time of year and whether some of the ingredients will be available and at their best; asparagus

that has travelled thousands of miles may taste stringy and bitter compared to the fresh asparagus grown locally. Eat seasonally as better quality produce will not only enhance the dishes but will also feel more in keeping with a theme: Hot Spiced Squash Soup from a flask is simply delicious enjoyed under the boughs of a great tree on a country walk, but perhaps not in high summer. Instead try a chilled soup like a gaspacho (adding ice cubes to the Thermos instead), to make the most of the summer's tomatoes.

And of course, you do not have to stick to the dishes I have chosen for each theme – you can mix and match or substitute in favour of one of your own recipes. But with this in mind, do think about whether the dishes work well together as a whole meal and will be as scrummy cold and served a few hours later.

If food preparation time is limited, opt for dishes that are easy and quick to make, such as the Spiced Citrus Couscous (page 28) or the New York Deli Sandwich (page 108). Gooey Triple Chocolate Brownies (page 74) are a doddle and can be made in under 30 minutes, and Salad Jars (page 40) look fantastic and are easily transportable.

And if you do not have time to make all of the recipes, consider asking others attending the picnic to contribute a dish or two.

Some tips to help you choose your menu wisely:

- Go for dishes that work well with the season, buying produce locally and organically.

- Consider your guests when choosing a menu. A four-year-old may find Gravlax and Horseradish Cream a little overbearing, while vegetarian Aunt Sally could be in for a hungry night if there are only meaty dishes on offer.

- You must have means to pack and transport your food safely, with emphasis on making sure all the food is kept cool and fresh (see Packing Your Picnic, page 86).

- Finally, consider how much time and help you have to make the food and keep the dishes simple if it is limited.

4 Luxe Picnic

This is the picnic for any special occasion, whether it be a for an intimate wedding breakfast or perhaps an evening under the stars at an outdoors concert, everything about the Luxe is oozing decadence and refinery. It is nice to get your best china, glass and silver out for this event. Table linen is a must, no paper towels here please! The dishes on this menu are simple and clean with a touch of refinery and flavours that pack a punch. And, of course, the menu is designed to make hosting a meal outdoors fuss free. This theme may take a fair bit of planning what with all the elements involved, but this is the ultimate way to picnic, and that ultimately leads to effortless luxury.

Gravlax with Gin & Beets

Buckwheat Blinis with Horseradish Cream

Summer Terrine Drizzled with Mint Oil

Porchetta

Salad of Truffled French Beans

Raspberry & Chocolate Ganache Tart

Fizzy Floral Cocktail

Gravlax with Gin & Beets

Any luxurious picnic party should start with a canapé or two and this scrumptious Scandinavian delicacy is a must for any celebratory feast. The salmon is easy to prepare and can be made well in advance. Serve it with Buckwheat Blinis and Horseradish Cream (see page 54) to keep picnickers happy while you unwrap and assemble the feast.

Line a large tray with clingfilm/plastic wrap before laying the salmon skin side down on the tray. Run your hand gently over the flesh and remove any remaining bones with tweezers. Pour over the gin and rub it into the flesh really well.

In a pestle and mortar or food processor, crush the seeds, pepper and juniper berries until they are fine. Add the sugar and flaked sea salt and mix well before sprinkling this evenly over the salmon fillet. Next, sprinkle over the grated beets and salt and spice mixture and then grate the zest of 1 lemon evenly over it too. Lastly, layer on the chopped dill. The whole salmon side should be covered. Lay another piece of clingfilm/plastic wrap over the top and wrap the fish tightly, keeping the fillet in the tray for any leaking juices to escape into. Lay a chopping board or heavy tray on top of the salmon to flatten and weigh the fillet down, then leave the fish to marinade in the fridge for 48 hours.

After this time, remove the clingfilm/plastic wrap and pour away the brine that is in the tray. Push the salt, spices, beets and dill off the fish and discard. Wash away any excess topping with water if you need to and pat the gravlax down with paper towel. Well wrapped, the gravlax will keep in your fridge for up to 2 weeks.

To serve, place the fish skin side down on a large chopping board. Using a sharp narrow-bladed knife, start at the tail end and separate the skin from the fillet. discard the skin and remove any brown bits of flesh from underneath. Now, with the knife on a diagonal slant, slice the gravlax into very thin sheets. Arrange on the buckwheat blinis with a dollop of horseradish cream and a tiny sprig of chives or dill for prettiness.

Vegetarian Alternative

If cured salmon is not your thing or you need a vegetarian option, a delicious alternative is to use cooked beets instead.

Preheat the oven to 200°C (400°F) Gas 6. Wash and peel 4 fresh beets. Keep the beets whole and place them in a roasting pan. Drizzle with olive oil, place a sprig of rosemary amongst them and season well with salt and pepper. Roast in the preheated oven for 30 minutes, then leave to cool. Slice very thinly into discs with a vegetable peeler or mandolin.

To serve, place a few discs of beet onto each of the blinis and spoon over a small dollop of horseradish or sour cream. Alternatively a crumble of strong blue cheese is wonderful with the sweet beets. Finally, top with a whole walnut and sprinkle with finely chopped parsley and chives.

700 g/1½ lb. piece of salmon, filleted
   but skin left on
75 ml/5 tablespoons gin
½ tablespoon fennel seeds
½ tablespoon caraway seeds
½ tablespoon ground pink pepper
1 tablespoon crushed juniper berries
50 g/¼ caster/granulated sugar
170 g/¾ cup sea salt flakes
2 fresh beets, peeled and grated
a bunch of fresh dill
grated zest of 1 lemon

To serve:
Buckwheat Blinis (see page 54)
Horseradish Cream (see page 54)
a handful of fresh chives or dill, for
   garnishing the blinis

serves 8

400 ml/1⅔ cups whole milk
½ teaspoon salt
300 g/2¼ cups buckwheat flour
100 g/¾ cup plain/all-purpose flour
30 g/1 oz. fresh yeast
2 eggs, separated
200 ml/¾ cup ale
butter, for frying

serves 8

2 tablespoons finely grated fresh
    horseradish root
350 g/1½ cups crème fraîche
a good pinch of English mustard
    powder
sea salt and ground black pepper

Buckwheat Blinis with Horseradish Cream

In a saucepan set over low heat, warm the milk very gently until it is tepid.

In a large mixing bowl, put the salt in the bottom, followed by the flours and lastly crumble the yeast on top. Make a well in the middle and pour in the tepid milk and the two egg yolks, whisking rapidly until smooth. Add half of the ale and mix well again to a smooth thick batter. Cover the bowl with clingfilm/plastic wrap and leave in a warm place for at least 2 hours to activate the yeast. It will double in volume.

In a separate bowl, whisk the egg whites until stiff but not dry.

Add the remaining ale to the batter, mix slowly, then gently fold in the egg whites. Cover again and let the mixture stand for 30 minutes or so.

Heat a good dollop of butter in a non-stick frying pan set over medium–high heat, and swirl the pan so the melted butter covers the base. Use a dessertspoon to spoon dollops of batter into the pan, spaced well apart, and fry until little bubbles appear on top. When the edges of the blinis are golden, use a palette knife to flip the pancakes over and cook the other sides for a 1–2 minutes. When cooked, transfer the blinis to a paper towel to soak up any excess grease and leave to cool. Repeat, cooking batches of blinis until all the batter is used up. Pack in an airtight container. They are best eaten on the day of making.

Horseradish Cream

In a small mixing bowl, mix all the ingredients together and season with salt and pepper. Transfer to an airtight container and and keep cool until ready to serve.

Fizzy Floral Cocktail

Luxe should always include bubbles and this recipe leaves the floral notes of summer on your tongue with every sip.

8 x 25 ml/1 oz. measures of gin
16 teaspoons (80 ml/⅓ cup)
    elderflower cordial
1 lemon
1–2 bottles Champagne

8 sprigs of whitecurrants
    (if available), to garnish

8 Champagne glasses

serves 8

Add a measure of gin and 2 teaspoons elderflower cordial to each glass. Cut the lemon in half and squeeze in a little juice, then top up with Champagne. Repeat for all the glasses, garnishing each simply with a sprig of whitecurrants to float around the glass – yummy to eat afterwards!

Summer Terrine Drizzled with Mint Oil

Summer is the best time for terrines when one wants something cool and refreshing on the palate that is a sophisticated change to a salad. What's more, a terrine is perfect for picnics as it can be prepared in advance, can be transported easily (make sure you leave it in the mould) and the presentation and textures can make a dramatic focal point to a meal.

Bring 750 ml/3 cups of salted water to the boil. Drop the asparagus and broad/fava beans in and cook for 30 seconds. Remove from the water with a slotted spoon and refresh in ice cold water, then leave to dry. Retain the boiling water.

Remove the stems from the chard and blanch for 30 seconds in the boiling water. Shock in cold water before placing in a paper towel lined sieve/strainer so there is no liquid left at all. Retain the water you have cooked the vegetables in.

Melt the butter in a very large heavy-based saucepan set over a low heat and add the fennel, shallot and garlic. Sweat until translucent, but do not brown. Add the star anise and coriander seeds along with the boiling water from blanching the vegetables and top up with another 750 ml/3 cups or so. You should have approximately 1.5 litres/6 cups of liquid. Simmer for 45 minutes. After 45 minutes the fennel stock should have reduced considerably. Strain the liquid and leave to cool a little.

Soak the gelatine leaves in warm water until floppy. Shake the water off the softened leaves and add them to the tepid fennel stock, stirring until dissolved.

Line the terrine mould with clingfilm/plastic wrap, leaving enough excess film/wrap to fold over the top.

Remove and discard the rind from the goat's cheese, if there is any, and put it in a small mixing bowl. Season with salt and pepper, add the lemon juice and zest and cream together with a fork.

Now start building the terrine. Start by layering the bottom of the mould evenly with half of the chard, making sure it is compressed down and pushed well into all 4 corners. On top of the chard, lay 12 asparagus spears in a layer, tip to tail. Spread over half of the goats' cheese and press down so the goats' cheese falls between the asparagus spears. Layer on half the broad/fava beans, and make sure they are laying flat. Now pour in enough of the fennel stock jelly to just cover the layers in the mould. Put this in the fridge for 20 minutes or so to allow the jelly to firm up before repeating the layering process, starting again with the chard and finishing with the jelly. By this point, the mould should be full. Cover the terrine with the overhanging clingfilm/plastic wrap and leave in the fridge for at least 6 hours to fully set.

For the mint oil, simply whizz the herbs in an electric herb chopper or blender with a glug of olive oil to a rough purée. Add this to the rest of the olive oil with a good pinch of salt and decant into a bottle. Leave overnight to infuse and shake well before serving.

Keep the terrine in the mould until ready to serve so it is easier to transport. To serve, remove the terrine from the mould by lifting it out by the clingfilm/plastic wrap. Serve with some micro-herbs to garnish and a drizzle of mint oil.

36 asparagus spears (long, thin and tender work best)
2 large bunches of chard or spinach
100 g/scant 1 cup broad/fava beans
1 knob of butter
3 bulbs fennel, sliced
1 shallot, sliced
3 garlic cloves, sliced
2 star anise
1 teaspoon coriander seeds
8 sheets of leaf gelatine
400 g/14 oz. goats' cheese
freshly squeezed juice and finely grated zest of 1 lemon
sea salt and ground black pepper
a small bag of micro-herbs, to serve

For the mint oil:
a bunch of fresh mint
3–4 tablespoons virgin olive oil

a 25 x 6 cm/10 x 2½ inch terrine mould

serves 8

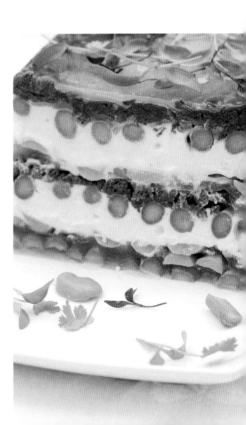

Porchetta

This simple Italian roast pork dish is a marvel. It's meaty, it's herby, it's rustic and it's just as delicious cold as it is warm, so perfect for picnics. Don't be intimidated by the name as it is quite easy to do if you plan in advance and make it the day before. See page 13 for my salsa verde recipe, which makes the most divine accompaniment to the porchetta.

First, make a herb and spice rub. Chop together the thyme, rosemary and sage leaves and put in a mixing bowl along with the fennel seeds, 1 generous tablespoon coarse sea salt and 1 teaspoon ground black pepper.

Lay the pork on a board, skin side down and make 10–12 short incisions over the meat. Stuff the cuts with slivers of garlic and then rub in the herbs and salt, making sure you work the mixture well into the slits.

Lay the sprigs of rosemary and bay leaves in a roasting pan and place the pork skin side down still, on to this. Cover and pop in the fridge for a few hours to infuse, or overnight is even better.

When it has marinated, preheat the oven to 240°C (475°F) Gas 9.

Take the pork out of the roasting pan and place back on the board. Gently roll the pork up into a log. If any of the herb mix falls out of the side, stuff it back in. Use the lengths of string to tie up the pork, not too tightly, spreading them evenly along the roll. Place the pork back on its bed of rosemary and bay in the roasting pan. Drizzle with olive oil and work this well into the fat before seasoning lightly with salt and pepper. Let the pork stand at room temperature while the oven comes up to heat, then place it in the hot oven for 45 minutes, basting every now and again. After 45 minutes take the pork out of the oven and spoon over the runny honey. Reduce the oven temperature to 200°C (400°F) Gas 6 and cook for a further 20 minutes. After this time, take out of the oven, cover in kitchen foil, making sure you seal the pan well to insulate, and allow the pork to rest in the foil covered pan.

You can now slice and serve or allow the porchetta to cool, slice and take with you on your picnic.

2 tablespoons of fresh thyme leaves

4 sprigs of fresh rosemary, leaves removed, plus 8 whole sprigs

1 bunch of fresh sage leaves, roughly chopped

1 tablespoon fennel seeds, crushed

a 2.25-kg/5-lb. loin of pork, off the bone (ask the butcher to remove the skin and leave about 1 cm/ ½ inch fat on the joint)

6 garlic cloves, sliced

8 bay leaves

3 tablespoons runny honey

coarse sea salt and ground black pepper

a drizzle of olive oil

6 lengths of string about 40 cm/ 16 inches long

serves 8

750 g/1½ lb. new potatoes or baby
   potatoes
220 g/8 oz. French beans
1–2 tablespoons caper berries,
   drained
a handful of fresh tarragon leaves,
   roughly chopped
2 small preserved black summer
   truffles (optional)
sea salt and ground black pepper

For the truffle dressing:
1 tablespoon white wine vinegar
1 tablespoon olive oil
1 teaspoon wholegrain mustard
 2–3 teaspoons truffle oil

serves 8

Salad of Truffled French Beans

One of the most luxurious ingredients in life is the truffle fungus.
A truffle has one of those delicious subtle qualities that can really
enhance a dish. Adding a decadent truffle to a rustic salad of potatoes
and green beans is one way to showcase the sublime morsel. I have
often seen preserved truffles in the specialist ingredients aisle of a
supermarket or in fine foods delicatessens. If you find a fresh summer
truffle then glory hallelujah, prepare to dine in heaven!

Bring the potatoes to the boil in a saucepan of salted water. After simmering for
8 minutes, add a steamer above the saucepan with the French beans and cook
both the potatoes and beans for a further 3 minutes. (The potatoes should have a
total of 10–11 minutes until they are cooked through.) Drain and refresh both the
potatoes and beans under cold running water until completely cool, then dry off.

   For the dressing, put the vinegar and olive oil in a jar or other sealable container,
add a generous pinch of salt, the wholegrain mustard, black pepper and finish
with the truffle oil, then shake together.

   Toss together the beans and potatoes with the caper berries and tarragon. If
you managed to find the black summer truffles, use a vegetable or truffle peeler
to shave very thin slices over the salad and toss through. Season the salad with sea
salt and black pepper and finally drizzle with truffle dressing just before serving.

For the pastry:

250 g/2 cups plain/all-purpose flour,
    plus extra for dusting
100 g/⅔ cup icing/confectioners' sugar
a pinch of sea salt
200 g/1¾ sticks unsalted butter,
    cubed, at room temperature
2 egg yolks

For the filling:

250 ml/1 cup whipping cream
200 g/7 oz. plain chocolate (70%
    cocoa solids), broken into pieces
1 teaspoon vanilla extract
1 tablespoon chocolate liqueur
25 g/2 tablespoons butter, cubed
200 g/1½ cups fresh raspberries

a 23-cm/9-inch loose-based tart pan

serves 8

Raspberry & Chocolate Ganache Tart

Well, we can't have a luxury picnic without something completely delicious, decadent and devious now can we? This tart consists of creamy chocolate wrapped in a light pastry, with a hint of raspberry to fling the flavours into another dimension. This can be made the day before an event and kept in the fridge but make sure you serve it at room temperature to allow the chocolate to relax ever so slightly and melt in your mouth.

To make the pastry, put the flour, sugar and a pinch of salt in a large mixing bowl, stir together, then add the softened cubes of butter. Using your fingers, lightly rub the ingredients together until the mixture resembles breadcrumbs. Now add the egg yolks into the centre of the mix and, using a spatula, work the mixture from the edge of the bowl into the middle until it forms a lovely dough. If the mixture seems too dry, you may need to add a tiny amount of water, ½ tablespoon or so.

On a floured surface knead the dough lightly until it is all shiny and smooth, then wrap it in clingfilm/plastic wrap and put it in the fridge to chill for at least 30 minutes.

Once chilled, roll out the pastry dough on a lightly floured surface to a rough circle about 3 mm/⅛ inch thick and use it to line the prepared tart pan. Cut off the excess pastry around the edge, then chill for a further hour in the fridge (or 20 minutes in the freezer also works).

In the meantime, preheat the oven to 190°C (375°F) Gas 5.

In a saucepan set over gentle heat, very slowly bring the cream to boiling point then remove from the heat and add the dark chocolate. Use a large whisk to gently stir until the chocolate is melted, then add the vanilla and chocolate liqueur. Stir in the butter, a little at a time, until melted, then leave the mixture to one side to cool.

Prick the chilled pastry case all over with a fork. Line the case with baking parchment and baking beans and pop in the preheated oven to cook blind for 15 minutes. Keep an eye on it and cover the edges with kitchen foil if they start to over-brown. Remove the parchment and beans and cook in the oven for a further 5 minutes. Leave the tart on a wire rack to cool.

Once cool, scatter half the raspberries into the pastry case and squish down with your finger before pouring over the thick chocolate ganache to fill the case. Chill for at least 2 hours before serving, giving the ganache a chance to set somewhat. You can either remove from the pan, slice into wedges (best to do straight out of the fridge and with a hot knife) and wrap each slice singly in baking parchment then in a sturdy box to transport, or leave the whole tart in the pan, wrap in kitchen foil and place horizontally in a cool box. Serve with the remaining raspberries sprinkled over the top.

5 Teddy Bears' Picnic

A picnic in the woods can evoke a thousand memories of childhood fun. I think of sunlight dappling through the trees, setting up camp and eating sandwiches wrapped in a hanky by the trunk of a tree. Within this theme there are plenty of dishes that will appeal to little palates as well as big kids. To create the look, collect odd bits of china typical of a tea party. Old vintage quilts and throws work beautifully as ground cover and, of course, the scene would not be complete without a few old bear friends for company. Think of some fun games to play with the children, or hold a competition for the best-dressed bear!

Sausage & Squished Tomato Rolls

Ham, Pickled Gherkin & Lettuce Wheels

Stuffed Potato Skins with Bacon, Cheddar & Sour Cream

Scotch Quails' Eggs

Cheese Straws with a Creamy Dip

Rainbow Slaw

Gooey Triple Chocolate Brownies

Banoffee Plant Pots

Homemade Pink Lemonade

Sausage & Squished Tomato Rolls

There is nothing quite like a good old sausage roll. Every children's party I have ever been to included sausage rolls. In fact, many an adult party, too. Though they can seem a little retro, sausage rolls are making a comeback along with all those other 70s dishes we thought were too uncool a few years ago. There are so many ways you can change a plain sausage and pastry roll. This recipe uses juicy squished tomatoes, but you could try a spread of wholegrain mustard or red onion marmalade, both of which are just as scrummy.

Preheat the oven to 140°C (275°F) Gas 1.

Cut the tomatoes in half, top to bottom, and scoop out and discard the seeds. Lay the tomato cups, cut side up, in a large roasting pan. Season well with salt, and pepper, sprinkle over the sugar and herbs, and drizzle with olive oil. Bake in the preheated oven for around 1½–2 hours. Leave the tomatoes to cool, then blitz to a purée in a food processor.

Preheat the oven to 220°C (425°F) Gas 7.

Remove the skins from the sausages and put the meat in a mixing bowl. Season well with salt and pepper, knead with your hands and put to one side.

Divide the pastry into 2 equal portions and, on a lightly floured surface, roll out each portion to a rectangle measuring about 32 x 10 cm/13 x 4 inches.

Divide the sausage meat into 2 equal portions and, also on the floured surface and with floured hands, roll each portion of the sausage meat into a long cylinder about the same length as the pastry, with the flat of your palm.

Spread the squished tomato purée over the sheets of pastry leaving a 5-cm/2-inch border around the edge. Lay a portion of rolled sausage meat along the long edge of each pastry sheet and gently roll up. When there is 2 cm/1 inch or so left to roll, brush a stroke of beaten egg along the inside lip of the pastry before finishing rolling up and sealing the edges.

Cut each roll up into 8 smaller rolls and lay them, seal side down, on the prepared baking sheet. Brush the rolls with the egg wash, pop in the preheated oven and bake for 15 minutes until puffed up and golden brown.

450 g/1 lb. small tomatoes,
on the vine
a pinch of sugar
2 teaspoons herbs de Provence
(optional)
a glug of olive oil
400 g/14 oz. good-quality pork
sausages
400 g/14 oz. ready-made all-butter
puff pastry
1 egg, beaten
sea salt and ground black pepper

a large baking sheet, lined and greased

makes 16

If you go down to the woods today,
You're sure of a big surprise.
If you go down to the woods today,
You'd better go in disguise.
For every bear that ever there was
Will gather there for certain because
Today's the day the teddy bears have their picnic.
Jimmy Kennedy

1 tablespoon cream cheese

2 teaspoons mayonnaise

6 sheets Swedish polar flatbread
or wheat tortillas

6 slices honey roast ham

6 iceberg lettuce leaves, whole

3 pickled gherkins, finely sliced
lengthways

150 g/1⅓ cups grated mild Cheddar

sea salt and ground black pepper

cocktail sticks/toothpicks

serves 6–8

Ham, Pickled Gherkin & Lettuce Wheels

These fun wheels are colourful and exciting compared to a bland ham sarnie. Hopefully the fun novelty of eating wheels will be an interesting diversion for kids large and small. This recipe uses Swedish polar bread, if you can get hold of it, otherwise wheat tortilla wraps work just as well.

In a small bowl, mix the cream cheese and mayonnaise together.

Take a flatbread and spread over a small spoonful of the mayonnaise in a thin layer. Next, lay a lettuce leaf on top, followed by a slice of the ham. Place 2–3 slithers of gherkin along the middle and sprinkle over a large pinch of cheese. Lastly, grind over a little salt and pepper.

Starting from one side, slowly roll the flatbread and contents into a tight log, using a few cocktail sticks/toothpicks to keep it in shape. Cut off and discard either end to neaten it up, then cut the cylinder into 4–5 discs, rather like with a sushi roll, removing the cocktail sticks/toothpicks as you go.

Repeat with the remaining 5 flatbreads.

Homemade Pink Lemonade

A picnic is not a picnic without one simple addition: pink lemonade. I've used traditional raspberries in this recipe, but if you would like a slightly mellower, sweeter lemonade, use strawberries instead.

250 g/8 oz. fresh raspberries (or fresh strawberries, hulled and sliced)

250 g/1¾ cups caster/superfine sugar

freshly squeezed juice of 8 lemons

1.25 litres/5 cups still or sparkling water

lemon slices, to garnish

serves 6

Whizz the raspberries in a food processor until puréed. Pass the raspberry pulp through a sieve/strainer, using a wooden spoon to push all the purée through, and discard any seeds. Add 50 g/⅓ cup of the sugar and a tablespoon of the lemon juice to the raspberry purée.

To make the lemonade, combine the juice of 8 lemons and remaining sugar in a large jug or pitcher and stir until the sugar is dissolved. Add the water and berry purée, stirring well. Garnish with whole slices of lemon and any remaining berries, then serve chilled.

12–14 small round new potatoes
4 rashers/slices streaky/fatty bacon
olive oil spray
150 ml/²⁄₃ cup sour cream
80 g/1 cup grated mild Cheddar
2 teaspoons snipped fresh chives
sea salt and ground black pepper

2 baking sheets, greased
a melon baller (optional)

serves 6–8

Stuffed Potato Skins with Bacon, Cheddar & Sour Cream

These little babies are great for getting your little babies into new and exciting flavours and textures. Potato, bacon and cheese are a great combination and the adults are sure to enjoy them as much as the little ones. These are served cold.

Preheat the oven to 180°C (350°F) Gas 4.

In a saucepan, bring the new potatoes to the boil in salted water for about 8–10 minutes until they are cooked through but still firm (al dente, as the Italians would say!). Drain them, then refresh under cold running water until cooled.

Put the bacon rashers/slices onto a prepared baking sheet and pop in the oven for 10–15 minutes until golden and crispy, then leave on a wire rack to cool. Leave the oven on.

On a chopping board, using a very sharp knife cut the potatoes in half. Gently scoop out some of the centre with a melon baller, if you have one, or teaspoon and put the flesh into a mixing bowl. Put the potato skin cups onto the other baking sheet and season with salt and pepper, then spray lightly all over with the olive oil spray. Pop in the oven for 12–15 minutes to brown and crispen up.

Meanwhile, turn back to the mixing bowl and add the sour cream, grated Cheddar and most of the chopped chives (save some to sprinkle on top) to the potato. Break the crispy bacon into small pieces, add to the bowl and mix well.

Take the skins out of the oven and leave on a wire rack to cool. Once cool, gently spoon a dollop of the creamy mixture into each potato cup. Garnish with the remaining chives.

Scotch Quails' Eggs

Bite-sized eggs are so much more fun than the full size variety and quails' eggs are packed with protein to keep the little ones running around all day. A nice way to serve them to the adults is to mix a little mustard with mayo and serve on the side as a dip.

12 quails' eggs
600 g/20 oz. good-quality pork sausages
1 tablespoon finely chopped fresh parsley
1 tablespoon finely chopped fresh thyme (optional)
1 egg yolk, beaten, plus 1 whole egg
1 tablespoon plain/all-purpose flour
4 tablespoons milk
75 g/1 cup fine breadcrumbs
sunflower oil, for frying
sea salt and ground black pepper

makes 12

Bring a small saucepan of water to the boil and gently lower in the quails' eggs. Boil for 100 seconds, then plunge the boiled eggs immediately into cold water to stop further cooking. Once cold, one at a time, roll each egg gently along a work surface with the flat of your palm until the shell is all crackled, then peel away the shell. Set the peeled eggs aside until needed.

Remove the skins from the sausages and discard and put the sausage meat in a large mixing bowl with the parsley, thyme, if using, and egg yolk. Season with salt and pepper and stir to combine. Divide the mixture into 12 equal portions.

Now get 3 shallow bowls ready, the first holding the plain/all-purpose flour seasoned with salt and pepper, the next with a whole egg beaten with the milk, and the last bowl filled with the breadcrumbs.

Take a portion of sausage meat and make a patty with it in your palm. Place a quail's egg in the centre and gently mould the sausage meat around it before rolling it into a ball between your palms. Repeat with the rest of the sausage meat and quails' eggs. Roll each scotch egg firstly in seasoned flour, then dip it in the egg wash before coating it in the breadcrumbs.

Pour the oil into a saucepan pan and bring up to smoking hot temperature, (around 180°C/350°F). Fry a few eggs at a time for about 4 minutes until they are golden brown all over. Transfer to a plate lined with paper towels to soak up any excess oil and leave to cool before serving.

75 g/5 tablespoons lard, chilled
and cubed

75 g/5 tablespoons butter, chilled
and cubed

225 g/1¾ cups plain/all-purpose flour

100 g/1⅓ cups finely grated
Parmesan cheese

½ teaspoon mustard powder

a pinch of grated nutmeg

1–2 tablespoons very cold water

1 egg, beaten

sea salt flakes

a large baking sheet, lined and greased

makes approx 24 straws

Cheese Straws with a Creamy Dip

Cheese straws are great to give to adults, kids and even toddlers who like to let the flakey pastry melt rather than chew chew chew. They make a great canapé or nibble to eat whilst waiting for the feast to begin and they are easy to make. You could always go a little wild and try a different cheese other than Parmesan. Gruyère works brilliantly for that lovely taste of the Alps, or even a hard cheese like Manchego would also be a splendid alternative. Yum!

Put the lard and butter in a large mixing bowl, add the flour and rub it into the lard and butter with your fingertips until the whole mixture becomes crumbly, rather similar to breadcrumbs. Add three quarters of the Parmesan, the mustard powder and a grating of nutmeg. Add 1 tablespoon of the very cold water and again mix together to form a dough. If it still seems a little crumbly, add another tablespoon of water – this should be enough. Bring the mixture together into a firm dough, wrap it in clingfilm/plastic wrap and leave it in the fridge for 30 minutes or so to chill.

Preheat the oven to 200°C (400°F) Gas 6.

When the pastry is chilled, remove it from the fridge and roll it out on a lightly-floured surface to a rectangle about 5 mm/¼ inch thick. Brush the beaten egg over the sheet of pastry and sprinkle over the remaining Parmesan and a healthy pinch of flaked sea salt. Now cut the pastry into finger strips about 1 cm/½ inch wide and 10 cm/4 inches long and arrange on the prepared baking sheet. Pop them in the preheated oven for about 15 minutes, until puffed up and turning golden, then turn the oven off and open the door. Leave the straws in the oven for a further 10 minutes so they really crisp up before transferring to a wire rack to cool. Once cooled, store the cheese straws in an airtight container until ready to eat so they won't soften.

Creamy Dip

100 g/6½ tablespoons cream cheese

50 g/3 tablespoons plain yogurt

2 tablespoons fresh chives, chopped
finely

freshly squeezed juice of ½ lemon

sea salt and ground black pepper

For the dip, simply combine all the ingredients together in a mixing bowl, add a pinch of salt and pepper and serve in a small bowl alongside the cheese straws.

Rainbow Slaw

Another nod to getting those little ragamuffins to eat some veg. This rainbow slaw combines delicious ingredients with bags of colour and texture. The creamy yogurt dressing, combined with fruit juices, adds a mild sweetness to the colourful strands. Hopefully the kids will love it as much as you do.

In a mixing bowl, combine the yogurt with the juice and zest of the orange, the lemon juice and the dill. Add the carrots, beets, apple and fennel and mix well. Season with salt and pepper and finally sprinkle over the poppy seeds to garnish.

2–3 tablespoons Greek-style yogurt
1 teaspoon finely grated orange zest
3 tablespoons fresh orange juice
1 tablespoon freshly squeezed
  lemon juice
a handful of fresh dill, finely chopped
1 carrot, peeled and julienned or grated
5 beets, peeled and julienned or grated
1 apple, cored and sliced into thin
  wedges
1 fennel bulb, halved, cored and
  thinly sliced
sea salt and ground black pepper
1 teaspoon poppy seeds, to garnish

serves 6

225 g/8 oz. plain (70% cocoa solids) chocolate, broken into pieces

225 g/2 sticks unsalted butter, cubed

3 eggs

275 g/1⅓ cups caster/granulated sugar

½ teaspoon vanilla extract

seeds from ½ vanilla pod/bean

135 g/1 cup plus 1 tablespoon plain/all-purpose flour

a pinch of sea salt

50 g/1½ oz. milk chocolate chunks

50 g/1½ oz. white chocolate chunks

a 23-cm/9-inch square baking pan, greased

makes 9

Gooey Triple Chocolate Brownies

Two words: chocolate heaven! Bake these brownies for 20 minutes for an über-gooey and rich delight, or leave in for another 3–5 minutes if you want them to be a little more crumbly.

Preheat the oven to 160°C (325°F) Gas 3.

In a saucepan set over a low heat, gently melt the butter and dark chocolate together, ensuring it does not burn, then remove from the heat and leave to cool.

In a large mixing bowl, whisk together the eggs, sugar, vanilla extract and vanilla seeds, then gently fold in the cooled chocolate and butter mixture. Sift the flour over the mixture, add a good pinch of sea salt and again fold together until well combined. Pour the mixture into the prepared baking pan and sprinkle over the milk and white chocolate chunks, pushing them down into the mixture.

Bake the brownie in the preheated oven for 20 minutes, until it has a crust on top but is still wobbly underneath. Run a palette knife around the edge, then leave the brownie to cool in the pan. Once at room temperature, turn out of the pan before cutting into squares.

Banoffee Plant Pots

I love making this dessert for the kids, who are sure to take utter delight in eating out of a flower pot! To add to the novelty you can put little edible flowers on top or sugared flowers sticking out. You could even play a game by hiding the pots around the picnic area and get the kids to hunt them out, rather like an Easter egg hunt, but a flower pot hunt! You can also make them in glasses, if you prefer.

Break the biscuits/crackers into the bowl of a food processor and pulse to a fine crumb. Alternatively, put them in a plastic bag and pound them with a rolling pin.

Gently melt the butter in a large saucepan, taking off the heat as soon as it is liquid. Pour the crumbs into the saucepan and mix well with the melted butter.

Put a small slice of banana in the bottom of the plant pot to cover the drain hole, then spoon the buttery crumb mixture evenly between the pots. Using the back of a dessertspoon, press the mixture down firmly, then pop them in the fridge for about 1 hour.

Whip the double/heavy cream until it thickens into soft pillowy peaks.

Divide the caramel condensed milk between the 8 pots, stopping about 2 cm/ 1 inch below the top of the plant pot. Over the caramel, layer a good helping of sliced banana and lastly spoon in a dollop of whipped cream to fill the pots right to the top.

This is the fun bit: use a knife to scrape the top of the cream away so it is level with the rims of the pots, then cover the top of the pots liberally with grated chocolate, which resembles earth. Garnish the tops with sprigs of mint poked into the cream to look like leaves and a sprinkling of edible flowers.

225 g/8 oz. digestive biscuits/graham crackers
120 g/1 stick unsalted butter
2 x 397 g/14 oz. cans caramel condensed milk or dulce de leche
300 ml/1¼ cups double/heavy cream
3 ripe bananas, finely sliced
175 g/6 oz. chocolate (preferably plain), grated

To decorate the pots:
a small handful of fresh mint sprigs
edbile flowers (such as violets or nasturtiums)

8 x clean 8 cm/3 inch diameter, 7 cm/ 3 inch high terracotta plant pots or similar sized glasses

serves 8

A picnic is romance in a jar and a wonderful idea for a first date as you can impress that special someone with your cooking prowess. If you've moved on from the dating stage, surprise your loved one with a thoughtful, handmade meal for two, hopefully with a few aphrodisiacs (but no garlic for obvious reasons!) thrown in for good measure. Nowadays, on Valentine's Day, eating in is the new eating out, so even a picnic on the living room floor is just as romantic as a candle-lit table for two. To set the scene you need very little for this theme: a picnic basket, a rug or blanket, some candles for when the sun dips down, perhaps your favourite tunes tinkling in the background, and most definitely a whole-lotta-love!

Potted Crab with Melba Toast

The Lobster BLT

Asparagus Wrapped in Parma Ham with a Lemon Mayonnaise

Basil, Mozzarella & Orzo Salad

Elderflower Pannacotta

Lime & Mint Spritzer with Cucumber Ribbons

Potted Crab with Melba Toast

Seafood has long been known to be a food of love and potted crab is no exception! Perhaps it's the buttery goodness that harmonizes with the creamy crab and the fiery paprika? Who knows, it just tastes like heaven. Melba toast works wonderfully to add just the right amount of crunch and texture. Don't forget to transport the potted crab in a chilled bag to keep it fresh and prevent the butter from melting.

Melt a knob of the butter in a frying pan set over low heat and add the chopped shallot. Very gently sweat down the shallot until it is translucent, but do not brown. Leave to one side to cool.

In a mixing bowl, combine the crab meat, lemon juice, a little grated zest, the paprika and a good pinch of salt and pepper. Once the shallot has cooled, stir it into the crab mixture and divide between the ramekins.

Using the same pan you sweated the shallot in, melt the remaining butter very gently. Once runny, pour the butter over the crab to cover in a thin layer. As the butter sets, press a few parsley leaves in flat for decorative effect. Pop the ramekins in the fridge for a few hours to set.

For the melba toast, first turn on your grill/broiler and toast the pieces of bread lightly on both sides. Remove from the heat and cut away the crusts with a sharp knife. With the bread flat on a work surface, slice the bread in half horizonally, sliding the knife between the toasted edges, and open up the slice like a book. Cut each piece into 4 triangles, then pop them back under the grill/broiler, un-toasted side up, to brown slightly and curl up. Allow to cool before serving with the potted crab.

75 g/5 tablespoons unsalted butter
1 shallot, finely diced
200 g/7 oz. crab meat (white and brown)
freshly squeezed juice and finely grated zest of ½ lemon
a good pinch of paprika or cayenne pepper
1 tablespoon fresh parsley leaves
2–4 slices medium-sliced white bread
sea salt and ground black pepper

2 ramekin dishes

serves 2

Picnics are very dear to those who are in the first stage of a tender passion.

Sir Arthur Conan Doyle

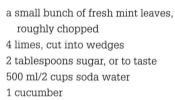

a small bunch of fresh mint leaves,
    roughly chopped
4 limes, cut into wedges
2 tablespoons sugar, or to taste
500 ml/2 cups soda water
1 cucumber

serves 2

Lime & Mint Spritzer with Cucumber Ribbons

No one likes to get too sozzled when in the mood for romance, so this mixology is without booze. If you do need a bit of Dutch courage, a measure of white rum takes this from mocktail to smooth-talking mojito beautifully.

Put the mint leaves in a large jug or pitcher, then squeeze in the lime wedges, dropping in the squeezed husks, too. Add the sugar and, using a wooden spoon or muddler, bash it all together. (Sometimes I even use a small wooden rolling pin to do this.) Pour over the soda water and mix well to combine. Taste and add a little more sugar if it needs it. Transfer to a thermos with ice cubes until ready to serve.

When serving, run a vegetable peeler along the length of the cucumber 3 or 4 times to get some lovely ribbons (discard the first ribbon, which will be mainly skin). Wrap the ribbons around the inside of two tall glasses before pouring the lime and mint spritzer over the top.

The Lobster BLT

This divine recipe sticks with the seafood theme but throws a hearty sandwich into the mix. And what is the best sandwich on the planet? Only a BLT club. With flaky lobster and a tangy mayo? 'Oh my goodness', I hear you say.

If you need to cook the lobster tail, simply cut down each side of the shell and peel it back to reveal the meat. Put 500 ml/2 cups of water in a large saucepan and bring to a simmer. Add the bay leaf, salt and pepper and a twist of lemon peel. Gently place the lobster tail in the water and cook over a low heat for 5–8 minutes. Keep a close eye on it and when the meat turns from translucent to opaque it is cooked. Remove the lobster from the water and leave to cool.

Heat a grill/broiler and cook the bacon until crisp and golden. Leave to cool.

In a bowl, combine the mayonnaise with the tarragon and lemon juice and zest.

When the lobster meat is at room temperature, roughly chop it and mix it into the mayonnaise, reserving a little mayo to spread on the rolls.

Split your rolls and toast the inside, then gently spread a little of the reserved lemon mayo over the toasted surfaces, as if you were buttering. Take the bottom halves of the rolls and start layering up the sandwiches, first adding lettuce leaves, then tomato slices (sprinkle a little salt and pepper over the tomato for seasoning). Spoon half of the lobster mayonnaise into each roll and lay 3 slices of bacon on top. Pop the top half of the roll on and devour.

For the lobster:

330 g/11 oz. lobster meat (1 large rock lobster tail is best)
1 bay leaf
a twist of lemon peel

For the sandwich:

6 rashers/slices streaky/fatty bacon
2 tablespoons mayonnaise*
2 tablespoons fresh tarragon, roughly chopped
freshly squeezed juice and finely grated zest of 1 lemon
1 beef/beefsteak tomato, sliced
1 baby gem/romaine lettuce, washed
2 bread rolls (toasted brioche rolls work well, as do soft white rolls)
sea salt and ground black pepper

makes 2

* Or you can use the lemon mayonnaise from page 82 and just add tarragon

8 spears of asparagus

4 slices Parma ham/prosciutto, sliced in half widthways

For the lemon mayonnaise:

3 egg yolks

freshly squeezed juice and finely grated zest of 1 lemon

150 ml/⅔ cup extra virgin olive oil

sea salt and ground black pepper

serves 2

Asparagus Wrapped in Parma Ham with a Lemon Mayonnaise

Asparagus is well known for its aphrodisiac qualities, and when you pair it with Parma ham/prosciutto and creamy lemon you will certainly feel the love. These flavours work so perfectly together, plus it is a quick recipe to prepare, contain and transport and will have you craving for more, oh la la!

Set a large saucepan of salted water over a high heat and bring to the boil. Trim or break off the base of each asparagus spear, then poach them in the water for 90 seconds only. Plunge the spears into ice cold water to refresh, then lay them on paper towels to dry off.

Wrap a piece of Parma ham/prosciutto around the middle of each asparagus spear, keeping the flowered head exposed. Keep them cool until ready to eat.

To make the lemon mayonnaise, simply whizz up the egg yolk, lemon juice and a pinch of salt and pepper in a food processor. While the machine is still running, very slowly dribble in the olive oil until it until it is all incorporated. When you have a lovely smooth texture, mix in the lemon zest.

Serve the asparagus with a sprinkling of black pepper and the lemon mayonnaise on the side for dipping.

Tip: If the mayonnaise starts to separate or go lumpy at all, add ½ teaspoon of white wine vinegar before resuming adding the oil.

Basil, Mozzarella & Orzo Salad

The Italians know much about love and I'm positive it starts with the food they eat. Rather like grass roots, love flows from the earth up and this dish is full of rustic charm, delicious ingredients and fresh Italian flavours.

In a blender, whizz up most of the basil (keep a few leaves back for garnish), the grated Parmesan, garlic, pine nuts, olive oil and a grind of salt and pepper to make a fresh pesto.

Bring a small pan of water to the boil, add the orzo and cook for 8 minutes or until al dente. Drain and refresh under cold running water before draining again.

In a large mixing bowl, combine the orzo and the pesto, mixing thoroughly, then add the torn mozzarella, chopped tomatoes and rocket/arugula and toss through. Lastly garnish with the last few sprigs of basil and a sprinkling of pine nuts before serving.

a large handful of fresh basil, roughly chopped

20 g/¼ cup finely grated Parmesan cheese

1 garlic clove

25 g/3 tablespoons toasted pine nuts, plus a few extra to garnish

1 tablespoon extra virgin olive oil

175 g/1 cup orzo pasta

150 g/5½ oz. buffalo mozzarella, torn

50 g/⅓ cup sun-blushed (semi-dried) tomatoes, roughly chopped

a handful of wild rocket/arugula

sea salt and ground black pepper

serves 2

100 ml/⅓ cup whole milk

400 ml/1⅔ cups double/heavy cream

20 g/1½ tablespoons caster/superfine sugar

3 sheets leaf gelatine

seeds from ½ vanilla pod/bean

2 tablespoons elderflower cordial

thin butter biscuits/cookies, to serve (optional)

fresh berries, to serve (optional)

4 individual pudding basins or ramekin dishes

makes 4

Elderflower Pannacotta

Although chocolate is meant to be the ultimate sweet aphrodisiac, it is also quite heavy. A pannacotta is light and heavenly and not too sickly. The summery notes of the elderflower make a delightful end to the meal. The recipe makes 4, but they will keep in the fridge for a good couple of days. Serve with elegant biscuits/cookies and your choice of berries.

In a saucepan, bring the milk, cream and sugar to a gentle boil and simmer for a few minutes. You want to just scald the liquid but you do not want it to bubble furiously. Take off the heat and allow to cool.

Soak the gelatine leaves in warm water until soft and floppy. When softened, shake off any water and add them to the warm cream mixture along with the vanilla seeds and elderflower cordial and mix well. Allow the mixture to cool completely, giving it a stir occasionally as it does so, then pour into individual pudding basins and refrigerate for at least 4 hours.

The traditional way to serve pannacotta is to turn it out, rather like a crème caramel, but you can leave them in the pudding basins as this will make them easier to carry. It is lovely on its own or you can serve the pots with thin butter biscuits/cookies, and a handful of raspberries.

Packing Your Picnic

So the day has arrived, the weather is looking fine, you spent yesterday planning and prepping all you could, and today is the day of your splendid picnic.

Packing your picnic correctly is essential and can save you time and energy, not to mention back pain from lugging around way too much stuff. Not only that, but if you pack correctly you will not be dealt the embarrassing blow of unpacking to find food has been squashed or spoilt.

It starts with your mode of carrying. This could be a stylish wicker hamper or a backpack, an Esky box or a wooden apple crate. Shop around for the best equipment and choose wisely depending on your theme – if you are heading out on a bike ride or a long country ramble, a large wicker hamper would not be very practical, whereas a backpack or saddle bag filled with food wrapped in foil or in lightweight plastic boxes would be much more suitable.

Do not be afraid to be a proud lover of Tupperware! It can keep food fresher longer, is light and easy to carry, and can be used for transporting liquids like soups along with more solid foods. Moreover, it is much lighter than glass or ceramic containers so easier to transport. And remember, you can always transfer the food to more visually exciting dishes once you reach your picnic spot.

If you are still not sold on the humble plastic box, there are other more visually quirky ways of transporting and serving food. Salads (see page 40) and desserts such as tiramisù (see page 22) look great in jam jars, and when all the food has gone and the sun dips down beyond the horizon, the jars can also be used as night light holders. Other things to try are tiffin tins, Chinese take-out boxes or even flat-packed paper boxes. These look great filled with sandwiches, cakes and other dry foods, which can be served on pretty cardboard pop-up cake stands to add a touch of glamour.

Both high-street stores and vintage markets offer a wide variety of picnic paraphernalia. China and glassware can look amazing on a beautifully laid-out picnic ensemble, but if you are not picnicking close to home or near your car, also consider plastic, paper or wooden plates and cutlery that are more lightweight and also conveniently disposable.

I find Esky boxes or cool bags a godsend if you need to keep things cold. Freezer packs can help keep everything inside cool, but you could also freeze bottles of still mineral water to act as cool blocks, which can then be a refreshing drink when they begin to thaw.

When packing, start with your freezer blocks at the bottom, then pack in your drinks (these should be cooled in a fridge first). Add heavier, bulkier food items and those in sturdy boxes at the bottom and lighter, smaller items on top. Secure the lid on the cool box or bag and do not open until you are at the picnic destination. The more the box or bag is opened, the sooner things will thaw out.

With food safety in mind, it is best to keep a beady eye on meat, fish and dairy products. Any food that needs to be kept cold should be kept in the fridge and added to the cool box only at the last minute. If you are barbecuing, make sure raw meat is kept separate from cooked meats and use separate utensils for handling them.

As well as the food (don't forget the salt and pepper!), there are plenty of other items that will come in handy – or are indispensable! Don't forget to take bin liners, paper towels and of course, something to eat off (see Setting the Scene on page 112 for ideas). Wet wipes are also one of those picnic essentials, as is a cork screw.

If you have space, an umbrella or gazebo is useful for protection from rain or sun, and suncream always comes in handy. Lobster is lovely to eat, not so lovely to resemble! A small first aid kit with antiseptic spray (useful for before and after prepping food) and plasters can come in handy, especially if you have kids with you!

Make sure you take enough picnic rugs for spreading out the food on, as well as providing a place to sit, or camping chairs to keep you off the cold ground. Pack extra blankets for when the sun goes down and things get a bit chilly.

7 Indochine Picnic

South East Asian cooking transforms fresh market produce into awe-inspiring dishes that send your tastebuds into overdrive. Asian food works so well for picnics as it can be made ahead, served hot or cold and is fundamentally cooked to eat on the go, outside, or at a little plastic table and chairs while mopeds and traffic whizz by. Obviously you can avoid mopeds and the hot slick city and opt for a quiet spot, laying out low comfy cushions and hanging paper lanterns to create a tranquil slice of Asia, wherever you are.

Vietnamese Summer Rolls

Salad of Soy, Wheat Berries & Cashews

Lemongrass Chicken Brochettes with Thai Pickled Cucumber

Sweet Chilli Noodle Salad with Crunchy Asian Greens

Caramelized Pork Ban Mi Baguettes

Exotic Fruit Salad with Fresh Coconut

Mango Syllabub with Passion Fruit

Watermelon Cooler

Vietnamese Summer Rolls

These fresh spring rolls are a far cry from the deep fried Chinese version we are most familiar with. Clean, cool and completely delicious, they are perfect for a summer's day and can be made the morning of your picnic and taken in an airtight container to be served straight away.

Break up the rice vermicelli into smaller lengths, about 8–10 cm/3–4 inches, and cook according to the package instructions. Refresh the noodles under cold water, then leave to drain.

Now get ready to roll. I think it's best to do this with an assembly line: start with a large shallow dish of warm water to soak the rice-paper discs in; next, you will need a plate covered with a clean tea/dish towel, on which to drape them once soaked; then the prawns/shrimp, herb leaves, vermicelli and other fresh ingredients, each in a separate bowl.

Soak a rice-paper disc in the warm water for 15 seconds until translucent and pliable, then move to the plate. Start to make a pile of the ingredients in the middle of the disc. I usually start with 2 whole mint leaves, placed shiny side down, then the noodles, grated carrot and bean sprouts, then 2–3 prawns/shrimp, and finally a good handful of coriander/cilantro (the trick to a good summer roll is not being shy with your herbs).

Roll up tightly from the bottom, fold in the sides, then finish rolling up the cylinder. Repeat the process for each roll, topping up the warm water when necessary. It is best to make each roll individually as the rice-paper discs tend to be quite sticky. Pack the rolls into a plastic container and keep cool until ready to serve, accompanied by the hoi sin dipping sauce.

25 g/1 oz. fine rice vermicelli
6 rice-paper discs or wrappers (available in oriental stores)
200 g/7 oz. cooked prawns/shrimp, halved lengthways if large
a bunch of fresh mint, stalks removed
a bunch of fresh coriander/cilantro or Thai basil, stalks removed
2 carrots, grated
30 g/½ cup bean sprouts
hoi sin dipping sauce, to serve

makes 6

Salad of Soy, Wheat Berries & Cashews

Wheat berries are a newcomer on the superfood street corner. If you have not heard of them, keep a look out in the special selection food aisle of your supermarket. Otherwise, they are easy to find online. Slightly different from barley or puffed wheat, these little babies have a firm and supple texture and hold their own with the soy sauce. The sweet roasted cashew nuts add texture and crunch.

Put the wheat berries and boiling salted water in a saucepan and cook uncovered over low heat for about 45 minutes, or until the berries are soft. Drain well.

In a large bowl, combine the warm wheat berries, soy sauce, oyster sauce and spring onions/scallions and allow to sit for at least 30 minutes so that the wheat berries can absorb the sauce. (You can make this the day before and refrigerate it once the wheat berries have cooled to room temperature.) Finally, stir through the cashew nuts just before serving so they keep their crunch.

200 g/1⅓ cups wheat berries
750 ml/3 cups boiling salted water
1 tablespoon dark soy sauce
1 tablespoon oyster sauce
4 spring onions/scallions, finely chopped
30 g/3 tablespoons roasted cashew nuts

serves 4–6

4 skinless, boneless chicken breasts, sliced lengthways into 3 strips
200 ml/¾ cup coconut cream
1 tablespoon soy sauce
1 tablespoon fish sauce
1 teaspoon Thai red chilli paste
2 tablespoons crunchy peanut butter
1 tablespoon sugar
freshly squeezed juice of 1 lemon
3–6 sticks lemongrass
Thai Pickled Cucumber, to serve

a metal skewer

makes 4–6

Lemongrass Chicken Brochettes with Thai Pickled Cucumber

This recipe is rather like the chicken satay you find all over South East Asia, sizzling away on tiny barbecues, the smell wafting down the street, making your mouth water. In this recipe, the lemongrass flavours the chicken from the inside, and cooking the chicken *en papillote* allows the chicken to steam in all the wonderful marinade juices. The cucumber pickle is the stuff of dreams. It is common all over South East Asia and is served with meat skewers of every variety. Leave the seeds in the chilli if you prefer a little more heat.

Put all the ingredients, except the lemongrass sticks, in a large bowl. Make sure the chicken strips are well coated with the sauce before leaving in the fridge for a few hours to marinate.

Preheat the oven to 180°C (350°F) Gas 4.

Take the metal skewer and thread it through a chicken strip before removing. Using the holes made by the skewer, gently push a lemongrass stick through the chicken strip. (You can choose to leave the lemongrass sticks whole if you like, but I find cutting the sticks in half lengthways makes it easier to thread through the chicken.) Continue piercing holes in the chicken with the skewer and threading them onto the lemongrass sticks until all the chicken is skewered.

Line a baking sheet with a large sheet of kitchen foil, with enough excess to fold over to create a foil parcel. When all the brochettes are ready, lay the chicken brochettes on the baking sheet, spoon a little of the marinade over each one, then fold the foil over and crimp the edges to create a sealed parcel. Bake in the preheated oven for 20 minutes. After 20 minutes, open the parcel, being careful not to burn yourself, and pop the baking sheet back in the oven for a further 10 minutes so the brochettes can brown. Serve with Thai Pickled Cucumber.

Thai Pickled Cucumber (Ajad)

4 tablespoons caster/granulated sugar
¾ teaspoon salt
60 ml/¼ cup rice wine vinegar
1 cucumber, halved and sliced thinly
2 shallots, diced

1 tablespoon finely chopped fresh coriander/cilantro
1 green chilli, deseeded

Put the sugar and salt in a saucepan with 4 tablespoons water and heat gently to boiling point, so the sugar dissolves and forms a syrup. Add the rice wine vinegar and leave to cool.

Put the sliced cucmber, shallots and chilli in a small bowl and cover with the syrup mixture. Leave in the refrigerator for up to 3 hours before using.

Sweet Chilli Noodle Salad with Crunchy Asian Greens

This dish is simple, fresh, extremely tasty and healthy. I love to make jars of the sweet chilli jam, and the recipe below can also be used with some other recipes in this book. If you haven't got time to make the jam, store-bought sweet chilli sauce works just as well. This salad is also delicious with king prawns/shrimp or langoustines added.

Fill a saucepan three quarters full with water and bring to the boil. Add your noodles and after 2 minutes put a lidded steamer on top with the bok choi, asparagus and mangetout/snow peas in. (If you do not have a steamer, you can cook these in a separate pan of boiling water.) Cook for a further 2 minutes (so the noodles get 4 minutes, and the greens get 2 minutes in total), then drain them together and blanch them all in cold running water. Drain again, then put both vegetables and noodles into a large mixing bowl along with the spring onions/scallions.

Combine the lime juice and zest, sugar, fish sauce and sweet chilli jam in a small bowl to make a dressing, then fold through the noodles. Garnish with fresh coriander/cilantro and sliced chilli, if using.

3 nests of medium egg noodles
2 whole bok choi, leaves separated
1 bunch of asparagus
50 g/2 oz. mangetout/snow peas
6 spring onions/scallions, sliced
freshly squeezed juiced and grated zest of 1 lime
1 teaspoon palm or brown sugar
1 tablespoon fish sauce
5 tablespoons Sweet Chilli Jam (see below) or store-bought chilli sauce
a bunch of fresh coriander/cilantro
1 red chilli, finely sliced (optional)

serves 4–6

Sweet Chilli Jam

10 red chillies, roughly chopped
8 red bell peppers, deseeded and roughly chopped
a 8-cm/3-inch piece fresh root ginger, peeled and roughly chopped
8 garlic cloves, peeled
1 x 400-g/14-oz. can cherry tomatoes

750 g/3¾ cups golden caster/raw cane sugar
250 ml/1 cup rice wine vinegar

4 x 395-ml/14-oz. jam jars, sterilized

makes 4 jars

Put the chillies, peppers, ginger and garlic into a food processor and whizz together on a pulse setting until the ingredients are finely chopped. (You could do this in a pestle and mortar if you prefer.)

Scrape the mixture out into a saucepan, add the tomatoes, sugar and vinegar and bring to the boil. If any scum gathers at the surface, use a spoon to skim this off before turning down the heat and simmering for 45 minutes. You will need to return to the pan and stir it occasionally so nothing sticks to the bottom. You will see the jam start to turn sticky. Continue to slowly cook for 10–15 minutes, stirring continuously. It should start to look like the inside of a volcano, a thick bubbling lava. Cool slightly before transferring to the sterilized jam jars and sealing, then leave to cool to room temperature. Stored in a cool dark place, the jam will keep for up to 3 months but will need to be refrigerated once opened.

Caramelized Pork Ban Mi Baguettes

Walking down a street in Vietnam it is quite common to see a street vendor selling baguettes, a legacy from when the French colonized swathes of South East Asia, called Indochine, in the 19th century. A Ban Mi is an eclectic mix of classical European ingredients – pork, pâté and baguette – with exotic Asian influences, including herbs, pickled vegetables and soy sauce. There are quite a few elements to this recipe but believe me, it is totally worth the effort.

To make the pickled vegetables, put the sugar and salt in a saucepan with 4 tablespoons water and heat gently until boiling, stirring until the sugar has dissolved and a syrup has formed. Add the rice wine vinegar and leave to cool.

In a small bowl, cover the cucumber, carrot, mooli, shallots and chilli with the syrup mixture and leave in the refrigerator for up to 3 hours before using. (You only use the vegetables in the sandwich, not the syrup, however this can be used for the pickled cucumber recipe on page 94, so do not throw away.)

Slice the loin of pork into about ½–1-cm/¼–½-inch thick pieces, put in a bowl and marinate with the fish sauce, honey, brown sugar, soy sauce, sesame oil, garlic, ginger and a pinch of black pepper. Mix really well and leave in the fridge for 30 minutes for the flavours to infuse.

Either on a barbecue/grill or in a very hot griddle pan, cook the pork slices for 2 minutes on each side until charred and caramelized, then leave to cool.

Slice open your baguette, splash soy sauce onto the inside and spread some pork liver pâté along one half. Place the pork slices on top along with the lettuce, pickled vegetables, a good handful of coriander/cilantro and mint, if using, and a sprinkling of sliced chilli.

300 g/10 oz. pork tenderloin
1½ tablespoons fish sauce
1 tablespoon honey
½ tablespoon brown sugar
1 tablespoon soy sauce, plus extra
   to serve
¼ teaspoon sesame oil
1 garlic clove, crushed
1 teaspoon minced ginger
a pinch of ground black pepper
2 large slices baguette
pork liver pâté, to taste
a handful of lettuce leaves
a bunch of fresh coriander/cilantro
a bunch of fresh mint (optional)
red or green chilli, finely sliced

For the pickled vegetables:
4 tablespoons caster/granulated
   sugar
¾ teaspoon salt
4 tablespoons rice wine vinegar
1 cucumber, halved and sliced thinly
1 carrot, very thinly sliced
½ mooli, thinly sliced
2 shallots, diced
1 green chilli, sliced

makes 2

Watermelon Cooler

A cocktail that cools you down, not only from the blazing sunshine but also all the chilli consumed on your discovery of the tastes of Indochine! If you prefer it to be sweeter, you could substitute the vodka for a white rum.

1 large watermelon, peeled and cut
   into pieces (reserve 6 triangle
   slices, skin on, to garnish)
125 ml/½ cup vodka
60 ml/¼ cup triple sec

freshly squeezed juice of 3 limes
ice cubes, to serve

serves 6

In a blender, whizz up the watermelon pieces, then pass the purée through a very fine sieve/strainer set over a jug/pitcher. (Discard any bits or seeds left in the sieve/strainer.) Stir in the vodka, triple sec and lime juice.

Either put crushed ice into tall glasses before pouring the cooler over, or put whole ice cubes and the cooler into a thermos to stay cold while you find your perfect spot. Garnish each drink with a reserved watermelon slice, to serve.

1 fresh pineapple, halved

1 fresh papaya, peeled and deseeded

3 sharon fruits/persimmons

10–12 lychees, peeled, halved and
    deseeded

3 bananas, peeled

freshly squeezed juice of 2 limes

60 ml/¼ cup coconut milk

3 tablespoons brown sugar

100 g/3½ oz. fresh coconut, chopped
    into chunks

a few leaves of fresh basil for garnish
    (optional)

serves 6

Exotic Fruit Salad with Fresh Coconut

In Asia sweet things tend to come in the form of fresh fruit, which is no surprise considering all the delectable delights on offer in that part of the world. Serving in a pineapple shell adds a rather retro twist to the classic fruit salad, while sweet coconut milk transports you to a palm fringed beach with every bite.

Scoop the centre from each pineapple half, keeping the shells intact to use as serving bowls. Discard the woody core from the pineapple and chop the flesh into bite-sized pieces. Chop all the other fruits into bite-sized chunks, discarding any seeds or inedible skin and saving any juice that runs out as you go.

Put the chopped fruit into a serving bowl or divide between the two hollowed out pineapple halves. Squeeze over the juice of 1 of the limes and any reserved fruit juices over the fruit immediately (this stops the fruit from oxidizing).

In a separate bowl, combine the coconut milk, remaining lime juice and sugar and stir until all the sugar is dissolved. Pour this over the fruit salad and garnish with chunks of fresh coconut and a few basil leaves, if using, before serving.

Mango Syllabub with Passion Fruit

I'm sure mango hails straight from the garden of Eden. A syllabub allows the mango to remain unadulterated so all that heady perfumed taste comes through, complemented by the ginger biscuits/cookies and vanilla cream. This looks fantastic served in glasses or jars so you can see all the lovely layers and sunshine colours.

Roughly chop the flesh of 2 of the mangoes, put it in a food processor and blend to a purée. Finely chop the flesh of the remaining 2 mangoes and stir the pieces into the mango purée.

Divide the ginger biscuit/cookie crumbs between 6 glasses or jars then spoon in the mango purée, dividing it equally between the glasses.

In a separate bowl, whisk the cream with the icing/confectioners' sugar and vanilla seeds, until it holds soft peaks, then add the lime zest and juice, and brandy. Spoon the cream mixture on top of the mango, then add a sprinkling of passion fruit seeds on top. This can be made 1–2 hours ahead but keep in a well chilled cool box or the refrigerator until just before serving.

4 large mangoes, peeled and pitted
6 ginger biscuits/cookies, crumbled
1 x 568 ml pot/2⅓ cups double/
   heavy cream
85 g/⅔ cup icing/confectioners'
   sugar
seeds from ½ a vanilla pod/bean
freshly squeezed juice and grated
   zest of 2 limes
4 tablespoons brandy
2 passion fruit

6 serving glasses or jars

serves 4–6

8 Woodland Walk Picnic

Autumn is a bountiful season, full of the produce of a late summer harvest. Trees hang laden with fruits and nuts and there are a plethora of squash and pumpkins along with the first root vegetables that will take you through the cold winter. This time of year is beckoning you to step out on a misty morning and head into the countryside to enjoy the golden colours of the fall and the last few rays of sunshine until winter takes hold with her icy grip. Wrap up warm in your favourite chunky knit cardigan and welly boots and head out for a woodland walk picnic. You could even include some foraging for wild foods: edible mushrooms, ripe blackberries eaten straight off the bush or cobnuts roasted on a small fire. It can be touch and go as to how damp the ground will be this time of year, so make sure your picnic blanket has a waterproof underside.

Spiced Squash Soup

Homemade Grainy Bread

Courgette & Vintage Cheddar Quiche

Salad of Roasted Root Vegetables

The New York Deli Sandwich

Salted Caramel Bites

Heavenly Gingerbread Cake

Hot Apple Cider

Spiced Squash Soup

There is nothing like a rich, heady, aromatic soup to warm you up on a cold day. This recipe is perfect to take with you on your woodland walk and the thermos flask can double up as a hand-warmer. Take a doorstop hunk of grainy bread (see recipe on page 104) to mop up every last morsel of this thick, delicious autumn vegetable medley. You can leave the skin on the squash or peel it – it's up to you.

Preheat the oven to 200°C (400°F) Gas 6.

Put the chopped squash and sweet potato and the whole carrot in a baking pan. Drizzle liberally with olive oil, season with salt and pepper and toss the vegetables in the oil to coat. Pop in the preheated oven for 25 minutes, until the vegetables are golden and tender.

Add a glug of olive oil to a heavy bottomed saucepan and gently fry the onions and garlic with the spices, cloves and cardamon pod. When the onions have turned translucent and glossy, add the roasted vegetables, stir a few times, then add the stock, the apple, a generous pinch of salt and a grind of pepper. Allow to simmer for 10–12 minutes before taking off the heat and allowing to cool. (You may want to fish out the cardamon pod and cloves, but they will have been softened by cooking and will be blended, so this isn't essential.)

Using either a hand-held blender or liquidizer, blitz the soup until it is thick and smooth, then stir in a couple of dollops of yogurt. You can now decant the soup into a suitable container and keep it in the fridge for a few days. For the walk, reheat the soup and transfer it to a thermos flask, which should keep it hot for a good few hours. Serve with homemade grainy bread.

1 butternut squash, chopped
1 sweet potato, peeled and chopped
1 carrot, peeled
olive oil, for roasting and frying
1 large white onion, diced
2 garlic cloves, crushed
¼ teaspoon ground turmeric
½ teaspoon ground cumin
½ teaspoon ground coriander
2 cloves
1 cardamon pod
500 ml/2 cups vegetable stock
1 apple, peeled and chopped
2 tablespoons whole yogurt
  (Greek-style preferably)
sea salt and ground black pepper
Homemade Grainy Bread (page 104),
  to serve

serves 4

650 g/5 cups wholemeal/
whole-wheat flour, plus extra
for dusting
1 teaspoon salt
1 teaspoon muscovado/brown sugar
25 g/2 tablespoons butter, cubed
2 teaspoons caraway seeds
1 tablespoon poppy seeds
1 generous tablespoon sunflower
seeds
1 generous tablespoon pumpkin
seeds
1 generous tablespoon linseeds
7 g/¼ oz. dried/active dry yeast
450 ml/scant 2 cups warm water

a baking sheet, lined and greased

makes 1 loaf

Homemade Grainy Bread

This delicious bread can be used in a number of ways. You could scoop out a bowl shape in the middle of the bread and when you are ready to eat, pour soup into the bread bowl for a retro treat. It saves you having to take bowls or mugs with you too! This is great for two people to share and once the soup is finished, tear open the bread and eat with gusto. Or you could use slices of the bread for the New York Deli Sandwich on page 108.

Sift the flour into a large mixing bowl and add the salt, sugar and cubed butter. Add half of the caraway, poppy, sunflower, pumpkin and linseeds and, using your fingers, rub the ingredients together until the butter is worked into the flour and it is all crumbly. Now add the yeast, pour in the warm water and mix together with your hands until the mixture comes together into a pliable dough.

On a well-floured surface, tip out the dough and stretch and knead for around 10 minutes until elastic. Shape into a circular disc and place on the prepared baking sheet. Score an X top of the loaf with a sharp knife and sprinkle over the remaining seeds. Cover with clingfilm/plastic wrap and leave in a warm place (an airing cupboard is ideal) to prove for at least an hour, until doubled in size.

Preheat the oven to 200°C (400°F) Gas 6.

Bake the bread for around 35 minutes until golden on top. If it looks like the seeds are getting scorched, cover the top of the loaf with a piece of foil or baking parchment. A good way of telling if a loaf is ready is to tap the base. If it sounds hollow, like a drum, it is ready. Transfer to a wire rack to cool.

100 g/¾ cup wholemeal/
  whole-wheat flour, plus extra
  for dusting
75 g/⅔ cup plain/all-purpose flour
50 g/3 tablespoons butter, cubed
50 g/3 tablespoons lard, cubed
a pinch of salt
1 egg yolk

For the filling:
1 tablespoon butter
1 large white onion, diced
2 courgettes/zucchini, sliced
  diagonally
175 g/6 oz. mature vintage cheddar/
  sharp farmhouse Cheddar, grated
3 eggs
200 ml/¾ cup créme fraîche
200 ml/¾ cup double/heavy cream
freshly squeezed juice and grated
  zest of 1 lemon

a 23-cm/9-inch loose-based tart pan,
  greased

serves 6–8

Courgette & Vintage Cheddar Quiche

Late summer courgettes, lemon and a really strong pungent cheddar, encased in flaky wholemeal pastry: you and your fellow picnickers will be walking on sunshine, whatever the weather!

For the pastry, sift the flours into a large mixing bowl and make a well in the middle. Into the well go the butter, lard and a pinch of salt. Gently rub the flour, butter and lard together with your fingertips until the mixture resembles breadcrumbs, then add 3–4 teaspoons of water and the egg yolk. Bring the mixture together until it is smooth and formed into a ball. (You could do this in a processor if you wish.) Wrap the pastry in clingfilm/plastic wrap and chill in the fridge for at least 30 minutes.

Preheat the oven to 200°C (400°F) Gas 6.

On a floured surface, roll out the pastry thinly to a rough circle and use it to line the prepared tart pan. Cut off any excess overhang, prick the base with a fork, then chill for 10 minutes. Line the chilled pastry case with baking parchment, fill with baking beans and bake in the preheated oven for 15 minutes. Remove the parchment and beans, then cook for a further 4–5 minutes, until the pastry is golden. Lower the oven temperature to 190°C (375°F) Gas 5.

For the filling, melt the butter in a large heavy-based frying pan and sauté the onion and courgettes/zucchini. When golden, spread over the pastry case and sprinkle over a good handful of grated Cheddar.

In a large mixing bowl, beat the eggs, crème fraîche, cream, and lemon juice and zest together, then stir in most of the remaining cheese (leaving enough to sprinkle over the top of the quiche). Pour the creamy filling over the courgettes/zucchini, right to the top of the pastry case, then sprinkle over any remaining cheese. Bake in the oven for 35 minutes, until the top is soft set and golden brown. Allow the quiche to cool before slicing into wedges to serve.

Salad of Roasted Root Vegetables

This hearty salad uses all those wonderful roots that are young, fresh and in season right now. I've included cubes of chorizo, but you can leave it out, if preferred. With or without the sausage, every mouthful of this salad is packed full of fantastic autumn flavours.

Preheat the oven to 200°C (400°F) Gas 6.

Put the chopped vegetables in a large baking pan, drizzle with the olive oil and honey, season with salt and pepper and sprinkle over the thyme leaves. Toss to coat the vegetables evenly, then pop the pan in the preheated oven to roast for 30–35 minutes, until the vegetables are golden brown and caramelized. Remove from the oven, toss again in the hot oil in the pan, then leave to cool.

In a small frying pan, dry fry the cubes of chorizo sausage until lightly browned around the edges. Leave to cool.

Transfer the cooled vegetables to a large mixing bowl, making sure you discard the outer layer or two of red onion skin as you go. Add the chorizo and a little of the chorizo oil left in the pan. Toss in the rocket/arugula leaves, crumbled goats' cheese and balsamic vinegar. Season with salt and pepper and garnish with a generous sprinkling of parsley, to serve.

2 beets, peeled and sliced
2 parsnips, peeled and cut into batons
1 red onion, skin on, cut into wedges
½ small celeriac, peeled and cut
2 tablespoons olive oil
2–3 teaspoons runny honey
1 tablespoon fresh thyme leaves
sea salt and ground black pepper
1 big of handful rocket/arugula leaves
1–2 teaspoons balsamic vinegar
75 g/2½ oz. goats' cheese, crumbled
1 cooking chorizo sausage (about 55 g/2 oz.), cubed (optional)
a handful of fresh parsley, roughly chopped

serves 2–4

4 slices of good rye bread or
  Homemade Grainy Bread (page 104)
6 slices pastrami
2 tablespoons sauerkraut
1 pickled gherkin, finely sliced
75 g/2½ oz. Gruyère cheese, sliced
sea salt and ground black pepper

For the Russian dressing:
2 teaspoons mayonnaise
2 teaspoons ketchup
1 teaspoon creamed horseradish
a pinch of mustard powder

cocktail sticks/toothpicks

serves 2

The New York Deli Sandwich

There is no place like New York in the fall. On a crisp, cool day, a walk or bike ride around Central Park to marvel at changing colours is a must. Another must in New York is trying the famous Reuben Sandwich from one of the city's numerous delis. This traditional sandwich has been given many makeovers through the years with plenty of variations. This is my little nod to the Reuben. Enjoy!

Begin by making the Russian dressing. Simply whisk all the ingredients together in a small bowl and set aside until needed.

To build the sandwiches, start by spreading a generous layer of Russian dressing onto 2 slices of the bread. Add 3 slices of pastrami onto each slice, along with a good dollop of sauerkraut and a few slices of gherkin. Drizzle over a little more Russian dressing and top with slices of Gruyère cheese. Season with salt and pepper and then top each stack with another slice of bread. Use cocktail sticks/toothpicks to hold it all in place, but remember to remove them before eating.

Salted Caramel Bites

Salt and sugar are two flavours that it may sound peculiar to combine but which work magnificently together. These are perfect for handing out to your guests and eating on the go – like little energy boosters until you reach your picnic destination.

In a saucepan set over a low heat, gently heat the cream, butter and sea salt together until the butter has melted, then remove from the heat.

Put the honey, sugar and 60 ml/¼ cup water in a separate saucepan, stir and bring to a rapid boil. Continue boiling until the colour turns to a golden brown, then remove from the heat. Carefully, pour the cream mixture into the bubbling sugar and stir well, then set over a high heat and bring the caramel up to 115°C (242°F). Remove from the heat, allow to cool slightly, then add the vanilla seeds and stir in before carefully pouring the caramel into the prepared pan. Let cool to room temperature before popping the pan in the fridge for at least 4 hours.

Tip the slab of caramel onto a chopping board. If it has gone a little hard in the fridge leave it at room temperature for an hour or so to soften. Cut the slab into chunks before dusting with sea salt flakes. Wrap the pieces of caramel in baking parchment tied with string or put in an airtight container to transport.

200 ml/¾ cup double/heavy cream
70 g/5 tablespoons butter
1 teaspoon sea salt
60 g/¼ cup honey or corn syrup
200 g/1 cup caster/granulated sugar
seeds from 1 vanilla pod/bean
sea salt flakes (such as Fleur de sel),
   to garnish

a sugar thermometer
a 20-cm/8-inch square baking pan, lined
   and greased

makes about 60

90 g/6 tablespoons salted butter
90 g/scant ½ cup caster/white sugar
a pinch of salt
250 g/2 cups plain/all-purpose flour
1 teaspoon baking powder
½ teaspoon bicarbonate of
 soda/baking soda
1½ teaspoons ground ginger
150 g/5 oz. candied ginger pieces
110 g/scant ½ cup treacle/molasses
110 g/scant ½ cup golden/corn syrup
200 ml/¾ cup boiling water

To decorate:
150 g/1 cup icing/confectioners' sugar
45 ml/3 tablespoons ginger wine
 (or hot water)
2 balls stem ginger, chopped into
 thin slices (optional)

a 900 g/2 lb. loaf pan

serves 8

Heavenly Gingerbread Cake

Whether it be a reminder of school dinners, or one of those sticky delights that came out on gloomy winter afternoons around Grandma's house, there is nothing like a slab of ginger cake to bring back a flood of nostalgia and, as with most things gingery, take the edge off the cold. If you want to go really all out, a light scraping of butter over a wedge of cake is divinely decadent.

Preheat the oven to 180°C (350°F) Gas 4.

In a large mixing bowl, cream together the butter, sugar and salt with an electric hand whisk until light and fluffy. Sift over the flour, baking powder and bicarbonate of soda/baking soda and mix well again. Add the ground ginger, candied ginger pieces, treacle/molasses and golden/corn syrup, then stir the boiling water into the cake mix. Using the hand whisk on a low speed, slowly combine the ingredients together until smooth and gloopy. Pour the batter straight into the prepared loaf pan and spread out evenly, then pop it in the preheated oven to bake for 50 minutes. Remove from the oven and allow the cake to cool completely in the pan.

Make the icing by combining the icing/confectioners' sugar with the ginger wine and mixing well to remove any lumps. Drizzle the icing over the top of the cake, then sprinkle over the stem ginger slices, if using. When the icing is set, slice into wedges and pack into your picnic basket.

Hot Apple Cider

A cold, crisp day calls for a warm stiff drink and a hot apple cider is just the ticket for a warming pit-stop tipple. If you have a juicer then try making your own cloudy apple juice to add to this lovely drink. With its perfect blend of sugary autumn fruits and heady spices, it really is all things nice.

400 ml/1¾ cups (hard) apple cider
100 ml/scant ½ cup cloudy apple
 juice/sweet apple cider
3 cloves
2 cinnamon sticks
1 orange, sliced

30 ml/2 tablespoons sloe gin
 (optional)
1 teaspoon sugar (optional)

serves 4

Put the cider, apple juice and spices into a lidded saucepan and slowly bring to a simmer. Turn off the heat as soon as it starts to bubble, then add the orange slices and sloe gin, if using. Add a little sugar, if it needs it, then pour into a flask for a lovely pit-stop warmer on your chilly autumn walk.

Setting the Scene

So, you've got your theme covered, you've chosen the menu, you may have started planning and prepping the food, and now comes the fun part of setting the scene. Personally I love this part almost as much as making and eating all the delicious food.

You can take along props to a picnic that will help set the scene and enhance the overall experience, but consider first where you are hoping to have the picnic as the location can act as the back-drop to your stage (see Planning Your Picnic on page 8). For example, the Romantic Picnic would be perfect situated somewhere quite intimate and private – I see perhaps a rowing boat on a lake or a spot under the boughs of a large oak tree. The props to add to the scene can then be kept to just a few well-chosen items, cutting down on stuff you need to carry – perhaps a lovely book of poetry, a vintage patchwork quilt to snuggle up on, or a few twinkling candles always add a romantic touch.

For the Woodland Walk Picnic you may not want to carry too large a load, so think about warm woollen knitted shawls that could double up as ground rugs. Simple things like hand warmers, welly boots or a small vintage wicker basket would all set the scene.

You may have an old Persian rug up in the attic that would set the Bohemian Picnic off beautifully. Poufs, deep cushions in jewelled colours and even draped fabric or strings of beads could add a wonderful feel to your table dressing. You could even state fancy dress.

That bunting left over from the village fete would look beautiful at the Vintage Garden Party, along with odd vintage china jugs/pitchers filled with wild flowers, or think about using candelabras or silverware at a Luxe Picnic.

Research themes on the internet: www.pinterest.com is a wonderful source for photographs and a wealth of ideas.

Trawl through flea markets, antique shops and car boot/yard sales, where you can pick up vintage picnic hampers, decorative tableware, fancy-dress stuff or even swathes of fabric for very little money. All these can add to your theme.

You could ask your guests to all bring along their own contribution to the theme: a teddy bear, those lovely paper lanterns that are a memento of their holiday in Thailand, or the set of tea cups and saucers they collected for their vintage themed wedding. Just make sure the picnic site is close to a car park if people are bringing bulkier items.

And how will you serve your food so that it is in keeping with your theme? Paper plates and plastic cutlery offer disposable convenience – and are good for occasions such as the Bike Ride Picnic, where space is limited – but you could also look for tableware that fits in with your theme. For the Indochine picnic, consider banana leaves as plates; wooden chop sticks also look great. Check the Stockists section on page 144 for suppliers of a wealth of quirky and innovative items to help transport and serve your food.

Lastly, nothing creates ambiance like music and lighting. If you plan on staying into the evening, use lanterns or solar lights to create a warm glow. Citronella candles might come in handy, too, if there are plenty of bugs about. If you are creating your own sweet music, take along a guitar and sing songs by a camp fire. If there are no musicians in your company, then an iPod and portable speaker will do the trick and help to create a magical and memorable occasion.

Many times on a dreary day, I find myself gazing out of the window and dreaming of Provence. The fields of lavender, the azure sea, the markets in every town selling bunches of white asparagus that stand like sheaths of corn, or tomatoes so red and misshapen they look rather like small red squash, but to eat they are warm, juicy and so sweet. However, you don't need to be in the South of France to enjoy a taste of the Mediterranean. Summer's harvest of produce and a warm sunny day are just what's needed for a Provençal Picnic. Pack a checkered ground cloth, a baguette or two and some cheeses, along with the recipes below for a sumptuous gourmet lunch.

Globe Artichokes with Aioli

—⁓—

Salad Niçoise with Roasted Vine Tomatoes

—⁓—

White Bean Dip

—⁓—

Mediterranean Bread

—⁓—

Chicken Rotisserie

—⁓—

Parmentier Potatoes

—⁓—

Frittata Lorraine

—⁓—

French Strawberry Tart

—⁓—

Bloody Caesar

—⁓—

Globe Artichokes with Aioli

4 globe artichokes
1–2 whole garlic cloves
¼ lemon, peeled
1 bay leaf

serves 4–8

The globe artichoke is not as frightening as it looks and the leaves are simply delicious dipped in hollandaise, aioli or warm melted butter. When you cook a globe you realize that it is also incredibly simple to do. The French always have it so right when it comes to food – they've kept this one a secret for too long! As well as a great picnic snack, this would make a wonderful canapé or pre-starter to a dinner party, too. I've stated this recipe is for 4–8 people; personally I think a single artichoke is enough for two to share. However you might love it enough to serve one each!

Take an artichoke and remove a few of the outer leaves with some kitchen scissors (especially if your artichoke has little thorns at the top of the leaves). Slice about 2.5 cm/1 inch off the top of the artichoke. Pull off any smaller leaves towards the base and on the stem of the artichoke, then cut away any excess stem, leaving up to 2.5 cm/1 inch on the artichoke. Repeat with the remaining artichokes, then rinse them in cold running water.

Fill a large lidded pot about 5 cm/2 inches deep with water and add a garlic clove or 2, a slice of lemon peel and a bay leaf. Insert a steaming basket, add the artichokes to the basket and cover with the lid. Bring to the boil, then reduce the heat to a simmer and cook for 25–45 minutes, or until the outer leaves can easily be pulled off.

Artichokes may be eaten cold or hot. If you are packing for a picnic then refresh the artichoke in iced water immediately after removing from the pan and allow to dry before packing in the cool bag.

When it comes to eating the artichoke, pull off the outer petals, one at a time. Dip the white fleshy end in the aioli. Tightly grip the other end of the petal, place in your mouth dip side down, and pull through teeth to remove the soft, pulpy, delicious portion of the artichoke. Discard the remaining petal. When all of the petals have been devoured, take a knife or spoon and scrape out and discard the inedible fuzzy part (called the 'choke') covering the artichoke heart. The remaining bottom of the artichoke is the heart. Cut into pieces and dip into sauce to enjoy.

Aioli

3 egg yolks
4 garlic cloves
freshly squeezed juice of ½ lemon
150 ml/⅔ cup extra virgin olive oil
a little Dijon mustard or saffron,
    to taste (optional)
sea salt and freshly ground pepper

To make the aioli, blend the egg yolks, garlic and lemon juice together in a food processor. Whilst blending, pour the oil into the food processor slowly and steadily, until it forms a thick sauce. The mayonnaise should be vibrant and yellow in colour.

Season with salt and pepper, blend briefly and taste to check the seasoning. At this point you can add a little Dijon mustard or some saffron to add a different flavour, if you wish, or just leave it as a simple mayonnaise. If you like it a little runnier, add a couple of tablespoons of hot water. Serve with the artichokes for dipping.

10 new potatoes, boiled and halved

225 g/½ lb. green beans, trimmed

325 g/¾ lb. vine tomatoes

75 g/½ cup Kalamata olives, pitted

2 tablespoons extra virgin olive oil

5 eggs, at room temperature

1 lemon, halved, for squeezing

4 x 175 g/6 oz. tuna steaks, 2.5 cm/
   1 inch thick

4 little gem/Bibb lettuce hearts,
   quartered lengthways

12 olive-oil-packed anchovies

a large handful of fresh basil leaves
   (optional)

sea salt and ground black pepper

a ridged griddle pan/stove-top grill pan

serves 4–6

Salad Niçoise with Roasted Vine Tomatoes

The Nice salad is an old favourite. It evokes memories of a warm breeze coming off the Mediterranean and sand in between the toes. I think this salad is the perfect tonic for a hot day. The colours, vibrant and rich, compliment the simple flavours that harmonize perfectly. In Provence they sometimes use artichokes instead of potatoes, so if you're cutting your carbs this is a great alternative. As this salad includes eggs and fish, make sure it is kept very cool until ready to serve.

Preheat the oven to 200°C (400°F) Gas 6.

Put the new potatoes in a lidded saucepan (preferably with a steaming basket attachment) and bring to the boil. After 10 minutes add a steamer above the saucepan with the trimmed green beans in. Steam the beans for 4 minutes, then transfer them to a large roasting pan. Add the tomatoes (still on the vine) and olives to the roasting pan and drizzle over the olive oil. Pop the pan in the preheated oven for 12–15 minutes.

Remove the potatoes from the boil (they should have had around 15 minutes total cooking time) and blanch in cold water to cool before draining and halving.

Boil the eggs for 6 minutes, then put the pan under cold running water for a couple of minutes to cool down. When cool, peel the eggs and cut them in half.

Transfer the roasted tomatoes, beans, olives and any warm olive oil to a dish to cool and squeeze over the juice of half a lemon and toss well.

Heat a ridged griddle pan on the hob or over a hot barbecue for 5 minutes. Brush the tuna steaks with olive oil and season really well with salt and pepper before placing the steaks in the pan. Cook for 3–4 minutes on each side, until the tuna is cooked through. (Although I love rare tuna, this salad is to be served cold so the tuna should be well done and flaky.)

Lay the lettuce leaves in a large container and scatter over the new potatoes and anchovies, then add the halved boiled eggs, green beans, roasted tomatoes and olives. You can either choose to keep the tuna steaks whole and place them on the salad, or I like to break them into flaky chunks and toss through. Transport the vinaigrette separately and drizzle it over the salad just before serving, otherwise the leaves can wilt a little. Sprinkle with fresh basil leaves, if using, also just before serving.

Simple French Vinaigrette

a pinch of sea salt

3 tablespoons white wine vinegar

4 tablespoons extra virgin olive oil

1 generous teaspoon Dijon mustard

1 garlic clove, crushed (optional)

To make the dressing, add a generous pinch of sea salt to the vinegar and mix to dissolve. Add the olive oil, Dijon mustard and garlic, if using, and mix well before sprinkling over the salad.

1 x 215 g/7 oz. can butter beans
1 x 400 g/14 oz. can cannellini beans
1–2 garlic cloves, crushed
3 tablespoons extra virgin olive oil
freshly squeezed juice and grated
    zest of 1 lemon
2 teaspoons finely chopped fresh
    thyme
sea salt and ground black pepper

serves 6–8

White Bean Dip

This dip works wonderfully with the Mediterranean Bread. Rather like a lighter version of hoummus, the zing from the lemon with the sweetness of the thyme is a delicious combination with creamy beans.

Put the canned beans in a colander and rinse them thoroughly under cold running water. Pat dry with paper towels, then transfer them to the bowl of a food processor. Add 1 of the garlic cloves and a healthy pinch of sea salt and whizz to a purée. While the machine is running, slowly pour in 2 tablespoons of the olive oil in a steady stream. When the mixture is smooth, add the lemon juice and more garlic, if you like, and blend again.

Transfer the mixture to a mixing bowl and stir in the chopped thyme, lemon zest and the remaining tablespoon of olive oil. Season, then taste and add more salt and pepper as needed.

This can be kept in the fridge for up to 3 days in an airtight container. Serve with chunks of Mediterranean Bread.

Mediterranean Bread

Even if you are not a 'baker', don't be put off from trying this bread recipe. Making bread is easier than you think and, dare I say, can get a little addictive, especially as the warm smells of bread in the oven fill your kitchen with mouthwatering aromas. There is something therapeutic in nurturing, kneading and baking bread. In this recipe, the bitterness of the olives combined with the creamy feta and sweet sun-blushed tomatoes is heavenly. It is delicious with the White Bean Dip (opposite) or you could simply tear off chunks and dunk in really good olive oil.

Combine the water and the yeast in a large mixing bowl then sift in the flour followed by the milk powder, sugar, beaten egg and lastly the salt. Using a spatula, mix the ingredients together thoroughly.

On a chopping board, roughly chop the olives, herbs, chilli and sun-blushed tomatoes and add these to the dough mix, mixing well to evenly distribute all those lovely flavours into the mix. Place a clean tea/dish towel over the bowl and allow the dough to rest for about 15 minutes.

Dust a clean surface with flour (you may need quite a bit as this dough tends to be quite wet) and gently knead the dough, stretch and pull, knead again and so on for at least 10 minutes. Pour a drizzle of oil, about 1 tablespoon, into the mixing bowl and return the dough to the bowl, cover again with a tea/dish towel and leave the dough at room temperature for 8 hours (I think leaving it overnight works best). If you are pushed for time then you can wait for the dough to double in size, which usually takes about 2 hours, but for best results (for all those lovely flavours to combine) the longer it is left to rise the better.

Turn the risen dough out onto a well-floured surface. Knead a few times, then cut the dough into 2 equal portions and return one of them to the mixing bowl. Sprinkle half of the crumbled feta cheese onto the dough in front of you and really work it into the dough. Flatten the dough out into a rectangle and cut it in half lengthways. With the palm of your hand, roll each half into a long sausage, about 55 cm/22 inches long and 5 cm/2 inches thick, then twist the 2 sausages together while also coiling the dough around into a tight circle. Repeat this process with the other half of dough in the bowl.

Lay the coiled loaves onto the prepared baking sheet, cover with a sheet of baking parchment, then the tea/dish towel, and leave to prove again for 1 hour before preheating the oven to 180°C (350°F) Gas 4. When the oven comes up to temperature, take the towel and parchment off the risen dough and bake the loaves for 25–30 minutes, until golden brown on top.

400 ml/1⅔ cups warm water

14 g/½ oz. dried/active dry yeast

625 g/5½ cups strong white bread flour

50 g/⅓ cup dried milk powder/non-fat dry milk

20 g/1½ tablespoons sugar

1 egg, beaten

2 good pinches of sea salt

180 g/1 cup pitted black olives, roughly chopped

a handful of fresh rosemary or basil, roughly chopped

1 large dried red chilli

200 g/7 oz. drained sun-blushed/half-dried tomatoes, roughly chopped

200 g/7 oz. feta cheese, crumbled

a large baking sheet, lined and greased

makes 2 loaves

1 x 2 kg/4½ lb. whole chicken
a pinch of salt
1 lemon, quartered
a few sprigs of rosemary
50 g/3½ tablespoons butter, melted
1 tablespoon salt
1 tablespoon herbs de Provence
1 teaspoon ground black pepper

a rotisserie oven or lidded barbecue/grill
(optional)
2 wooden skewers (optional)

serves 6

Chicken Rotisserie

In Provence a rotisserie chicken is as common as a warm balmy day. Whenever in France, we buy a warm rotisserie chicken from the market along with a tub of parmentier potatoes and a bottle of chilled rosé before heading off to find a secret spot and gorge on our feast.

Season the inside of the chicken with the salt and stuff with the lemon quarters and rosemary sprigs. Pierce the chicken onto a rotisserie set up on a lidded barbecue or in a rotisserie oven. Set the heat to high and cook for 10 minutes.

During that time, quickly mix together the butter, 1 tablespoon of salt, the herbs de Provence and pepper. Turn the barbecue/rotisserie oven down to medium and baste the chicken with the butter mixture. Close the lid/oven and cook for 1–1½ hours, basting occasionally. Remove from the rotisserie and let stand for 10 to 15 minutes before cutting into pieces and serving.

Alternatively, if you do not have access to a rotisserie, a spatch-cock chicken is just as good! Take the bird and, with the skin side down, cut along both sides of the backbone and remove the bone. Press down firmly and open the chicken up like a book. You should find the diamond-shaped breastbone. With a pairing knife, cut along both sides of the breastbone. Run your fingers along either side and just pull it out. Thread two wooden skewers in an X shape through from thigh to wing to keep the bird in shape while cooking.

Preheat the oven to 220°C (425°F) Gas 7. Lay your chicken, skin side up, on a pan lined with foil and baste it well with the melted butter. Rub in the herbs de Provence and tuck in the lemon wedges around and underneath the bird and add a few sprigs of rosemary torn into a couple of pieces, tucking them between the leg and breast. Cook for about 45 minutes, the chicken should be crisp skinned and tender. Take the chicken out of the oven and allow to cool. Pour any juices remaining in the pan over the parmentier potatoes (see below).

1 tablespoon sunflower oil
1 kg/2¼ lb. waxy potatoes, peeled
and cut into 2.5-cm/1-inch cubes
a generous knob of butter (melted)
any juices or fat leftover from the
cooking the chicken
2 sprigs of fresh rosemary, stalks
removed and needles finely
chopped
sea salt and ground black pepper

a rotisserie oven or lidded barbecue/grill
(optional)

serves 6

Parmentier Potatoes

In Provence most 'charcuteries' and markets sell big vats of golden parmentier potatoes, sizzling away under the rotisserie to take home by the tub full. If you have a rotisserie, you could also roast these in a pan underneath the chicken to catch all the lovely juices.

Preheat the oven to 200°C (400°F) Gas 6.

Heat the oil in a large frying pan set over a moderate heat. Add the potatoes and cook for about 10 minutes, stirring occasionally to prevent them browning or sticking to the pan. Transfer the fried potatoes to a large roasting pan and mix in the melted butter and any juices leftover from cooking the chicken. Sprinkle with the rosemary and season with salt and pepper. Put the pan in the preheated oven and roast the potatoes for 30–40 minutes, shaking the pan occasionally to prevent sticking. When the potatoes are golden roasted, remove from the heat and serve immediately or allow to cool before packing them in an airtight container, ready for the picnic.

8 rashers/slices smoked streaky/
  fatty bacon
1 small shallot, finely diced
1 teaspoon olive oil
8 eggs
200 ml/¾ cup crème fraîche
75 g/¾ cup grated Gruyère cheese
sea salt and ground black pepper

a 20 x 28-cm/8 x 11-inch roasting pan

serves 6

Frittata Lorraine

This little number is an alternative to Quiche Lorraine, which can tend to be quite heavy and bland. Dispensing with the pastry, a frittata allows all the flavours to burst forward. Light, tasty and perfect to take on a picnic – after this I think you may well refrain from the pastry version for a good while.

Preheat the oven to 180°C (350°F) Gas 4.

Scrunch a sheet of baking parchment into a ball and then flatten it out (this will make it more malleable) and use to line the roasting pan.

Put the bacon in a large frying pan with the shallots and the olive oil and cook over a medium heat. Stir occasionally until golden and beginning to crisp up.

In a large jug/pitcher or bowl, whisk together the eggs and crème fraîche, then stir in the bacon, shallots and any fat from the pan. Add most of the Gruyère (saving a little to sprinkle on top) and season well with salt and pepper.

Pour the mixture into the prepared pan, sprinkle with the remaining Gruyère and bake in the preheated oven for 30–35 minutes until golden and set. You can eat it warm, or leave to cool, slice into wedges and pack into your cool box.

Bloody Caesar

The Caesar cocktail was created in Canada and apparently remains a Canadian drink, although I think it works marvelously well with this Provençal picnic due to the rich spicy tomato flavours. Although the drink is similar to a Bloody Mary, the Clamato juice (tomato juice flavoured with clams) gives it a completely, and much better, taste. Seafood restaurants in Canada often add a shrimp as an additional garnish, along with pickled French beans instead of celery. Mott's Clamato juice is quite easy to find in good grocers and online.

30 ml/1 oz. vodka, Grey Goose preferably
150 ml/²⁄₃ cup Mott's Clamato juice
4 dashes Worcestershire sauce
3 dashes Tabasco
1 lime, cut into 4 wedges
1 teaspoon celery stalk
celery salt, to garnish (optional)

serves 1

Pour the vodka and Clamato juice into a thermos filled with ice cubes. Add 4 or so dashes of Worcestershire sauce and 3 of Tabasco and a good squeeze of lime before popping the lid on and transporting to your picnic. Add a celery stalk and a lime wedge to serve.

If you are making this at home, serve in a tall crushed-ice filled glass, rimmed with a lime wedge, then frosted with celery salt.

375 g/12 oz. ready-made all-butter
shortcrust pastry

550 g/18 oz. small strawberries,
hulled and halved

3 tablespoons redcurrant jelly

For the crème pâtissière:

350 ml/1½ cups whole milk

1 vanilla pod/bean, split lengthways

4 large egg yolks

100 g/½ cup golden caster/natural
cane sugar

25 g/3 tablespoons plain/all-purpose
flour

grated zest of 1 lemon

a 23-cm/9-inch loose-based fluted tart
pan

serves 6–8

French Strawberry Tart

Oh, the delights of a French pâtisserie! Everywhere one looks there are tarts and pastries that glisten like jewels. Luckily a strawberry tart is one of those recipes that never really changes and is rather like a little black dress: it never goes out of fashion and always gets a wow. This strawberry tart recipe is simple to make and completely delicious with the strawberries and cream flavour.

On a lightly floured surface, roll out the pastry to about 5 mm/¼ inch thick and use it to line the tart pan, trimming away any excess pastry. Prick the base of the pastry case with a fork, then pop the pan in the fridge to chill for 30 minutes while you make the crème pâtissière.

Preheat the oven to 180°C (350°F) Gas 4.

Put the milk and vanilla pod/bean in a saucepan set over a medium–high heat. When the milk comes to the boil, turn off the heat and leave to cool a little.

In a large bowl, whisk the egg yolks and sugar for around 10 minutes until light and fluffy, then beat in the flour and lemon zest.

Pour the warm milk slowly through a sieve/strainer into the egg mixture a little at a time, whisking between each addition. Pour the mixture back into the saucepan and bring to the boil again over a low heat stirring all the while until it thickens. Take off the heat and allow the crème pâtissière to cool.

Now back to the pastry, which has been cooling in the fridge. Line the pastry case with baking parchment and fill with baking beans. Put the pan on a baking sheet and blind-bake for 15 minutes in the preheated oven. Remove the beans and parchment and cook for a further 10 minutes until golden. If you notice the edges starting to brown too much, cover them with kitchen foil. Leave for 5 minutes to cool, then pop the pastry case out of the pan sides (leave the base on the bottom of the tart) and transfer to a wire rack to cool completely.

When the pastry is cool, spoon the crème pâtissière into the tart case and spread evenly. Arrange the strawberry halves over the tart, starting in the middle and layering concentric rings all the way to the edge until all the crème pâtissière is covered.

Finally, warm the redcurrant jelly with 2 tablespoons water until melted, and brush over the strawberries with a pastry brush and leave to set for 2 minutes. Pop the tart back into the pan (this makes it easier to carry) and pack carefully into your cool box, or slice into portions and pack singly in sturdy boxes.

10 Beach Barbecue

When summer is in full swing, lazy days on the beach are just the excuse for a barbecued feast. Your barbecue could be an old trusty, a metal bucket or even a disposable one; once those coals are stoked the smell of the grilled food will draw them all in. The recipes for the beach picnic are championing the abundance of seasonal produce and packing a punch with all the different summer flavours. As the sun dips down on the horizon, get the fire stoked up and bring out some warm blankets. If someone in the party can play a guitar then all the better, otherwise camp-fire songs work just as well between mouthfuls.

Scallops Cooked in their Shells with Thai Juices

Rosemary Skewered Sausages

Lemon, Garlic & Chilli Potato Salad

Langoustines with Harissa Mayo

Tennessee Boozy Campfire Chicken

Tabbouleh Salad with Feta

Cornbread with Mango Guacamole

Baked Banana Splits with Peanut Butter & Chocolate

Cowboys' Hot Toddies

Scallops Cooked in their Shells with Thai Juices

This dish works brilliantly as an aperitif. After all that paddling around on surfboards or using up energy simply soaking up the sun, these little babies are a scrumptious appetizer before the main event. Scallops are such a luxury, yet they can be quite inexpensive when bought in season. Look out for scallops that have been harvested by hand-diving as these are more environmentally sustainable than those that have been dredged from the sea bed. Just a single king scallop or sea scallop is enough to sate an appetite and the sweet versus salty Thai juices are the icing on the cake. Be very careful, the shells do get extremely hot on the barbecue, so keep fingers away until they are cool enough to handle.

100 ml/⅓ cup rice wine vinegar
100 g/½ cup sugar
⅓ a cucumber, finely diced
1 shallot, finely diced
1 small red chilli
½ teaspoon salt
6 large scallops, in their shells
a small handful fresh coriander/
    cilantro, chopped
sea salt and ground black pepper

a barbecue/grill

serves 6

Put the vinegar, sugar and 60 ml/¼ cup water in a saucepan and bring to the boil, then gently simmer until it is a syrupy consistency, but not too thick. Add more vinegar and a little more sugar if it becomes too gloopy. Let the syrup cool, then add the cucumber, shallot, chilli and salt. Pour the sauce into a lidded jar. It is best to make and use this sauce on the same day, but it doesn't hurt to keep it in the fridge or cooler until ready to use.

If the scallops need preparing, use a spoon to remove them from the shell (reserve the shells) and clean thoroughly by removing the frill, the black stomach sack and any other debris. (You could get your fishmonger to do this for you). You can then put the scallops back in their shells and wrap up well in a layer of parchment paper and then cling film/plastic wrap. As with all seafood, they must be kept at a very cool temperature until you are ready to cook them, so make sure they are next to the ice packs and well chilled in a cool box before grilling. Place 6 shell halves onto a very hot barbecue/grill or straight onto the burning coals – the hotter the shells get the better. Now season the scallops and place one into each curve of the very hot shells, then place the other 6 shell halves on top to act as a lid. Cook for 3 minutes before turning the shells over and cooking on the other side for a further 2–3 minutes. Remove the shells from the heat and arrange on a serving platter.

Take the top shell lid off all the scallops, gently spoon over some of the Thai sauce and sprinkle over some chopped coriander/cilantro. If you simply can't wait to gobble the scallop down, use a fork to spear the scallop and eat with gusto before waiting for the shell to cool enough to knock the juices back.

Why do we love the sea? It is because it has some potent power to make us think things we like to think.

Robert Henri

12 pork sausages of your choice
12 long sprigs of fresh rosemary
1 tablespoon olive oil
chunks of baguette, to serve
French mustard, to serve (optional)

a barbecue/grill
a metal or wooden skewer

serves 6

Rosemary Skewered Sausages

All hail the British banger! A sausage is synonymous with a barbecue but this recipe gives it a bit of a kick by infusing the flavours of fresh rosemary right into the heart of every sausage. Most important here is making sure you buy decent sausages, so the flavours don't get lost in bucket loads of fat. Lastly make sure you have a baguette to hand to wrap around the sausage – and some decent mustard wouldn't go amiss either!

Take a sausage and spear it lengthways with the skewer. Remove the skewer and slowly thread a rosemary branch through where the hole has been made. If the rosemary breaks do not worry, just thread the rest of the sprig into the sausage from the other side.

Repeat this process with the rest of the sausages and rosemary sprigs, then brush them with olive oil. Place the sausages on a hot barbecue/grill and cook for 10–15 minutes, turning occasionally to brown on all sides.

Serve the sausages in a torn baguette with some good French mustard, if liked, or simply hot off the barbecue.

Lemon, Garlic & Chilli Potato Salad

The potato salad is one of those all-time favourites at any picnic, and this version is no exception. I came across a similar salad to this when I was in Australia and I thought the flavours were lighter and tastier than the original mayonnaise version. The chilli packs a punch with heat while the cooling lemon and herbs mingle with the garlic butter. Simply delicious.

Thoroughly wash the new potatoes under cold running water to remove any dirt, then put them in a large saucepan of water and bring to the boil. Cook for about 15–20 minutes, until the potatoes are tender.

While the potatoes are cooking, put the butter, garlic, lemon juice and chilli in a small bowl and mix well.

Strain the potatoes and transfer them to a large mixing bowl, halving and quartering them as you go. Add the butter mixture to the bowl while the potatoes are still warm and gently stir to coat the potatoes in the butter. When the potatoes have cooled, sprinkle over the lemon zest and fresh herbs, season with salt and a little pepper and mix well again to thoroughly combine.

1 kg/2¼ lb. new potatoes, unpeeled
100 g/6½ tablespoons butter, softened
2 garlic cloves, crushed
freshly squeezed juice and grated zest of 2 lemons
1 long green chilli, finely diced
a small handful of fresh flatleaf parsley, roughly chopped
a small handful of fresh chives, roughly chopped
sea salt and ground black pepper

serves 6

24 langoustines

a chunk of baguette, to serve

For the harissa mayo:

150 g/⅔ cup mayonnaise

1 garlic clove, crushed

2 teaspoons harissa paste

a small handful of fresh mint,
finely chopped

freshly squeezed juice of 2 limes
and grated zest of 1 lime

a barbecue/grill

a lobster pick or wooden cocktail sticks/
toothpicks

serves 6

Langoustines with Harissa Mayo

Similar to scampi, langoustines are actually a member of the lobster family. Unfortunately, due to over-fishing they are quite rare but if you do find them they make a delicious treat. Unlike other crustaceans, langoustines are already pink before cooking. Their shells are rather primeval, with spiky ridges and long knobbed claws. You are more likely to find langoustines already cooked, but if you do find them still alive they should be cooked as soon as possible. If you cannot find langoustines, lobster tails or large tiger prawns/shrimp make an equally delicious alternative.

You are more likely to find cooked langoustines over raw. With this in mind you will need to gently reheat them, but not cook them as this will toughen them up. Simply place them straight onto the outer edge of the barbecue/grill and cook for about 1 minute on one side, then turn them over and cook for 30 seconds on the other side. If you do manage to find raw ones, cook for 4 minutes on each side.

For the mayo, combine all the ingredients and mix well. Serve a dollop on the side of the langoustines and chunks of bread to mop up the juices.

To eat a langoustine, first break the head and thorax off the langoustine and discard. Peel off the shell around the tail and eat, then crack the claws to get to the juicy meat inside. You may find a lobster pick is useful but I also find a wooden cocktail stick/toothpick works just as well.

Tennessee Boozy Campfire Chicken

A barbie on the beach should include a bottle of bourbon, and as you can see with this picnic theme, Tennessee whiskey features several times throughout the menu!

Put the chicken in a sealable plastic bag. Using a rolling pin (or the side of the whiskey bottle works just as well!), tenderize the chicken by pounding it until it flattens. Open the bag up and add the bourbon, sugar, soy sauce, sesame oil, garlic and lemon juice. Season well with salt and pepper, then seal up the bag and shake it well to let the ingredients infuse. Put the sealed bag in the fridge for up to 8 hours to marinate or leave in a cooler for 1–2 hours if you are pushed for time and want to head to the beach.

When ready to cook, lay the marinated chicken on a hot barbecue/grill. Cook over a high heat for about 8 minutes on each side, or until cooked through.

If you wish, and have a camping stove, you can cook down any marinade left in the bag to serve drizzled over the chicken, although the chicken is still very tasty without this step. Simply pour it into a small pan and bring to the boil over the stove. Simmer for the same duration as the chicken takes to cook, until it thickens, then, when ready, spoon a little of the sauce over each chicken piece and serve.

6 boneless chicken breasts, skin on
200 ml/¾ cup bourbon whiskey
3 tablespoons soft brown sugar
2 tablespoons dark soy sauce
1 tablespoon sesame oil
1 garlic clove, crushed
freshly squeezed juice of 1 lemon
sea salt and ground black pepper

a barbecue/grill
a camping stove (optional)

serves 6

Tabbouleh Salad with Feta

Sometimes less is more, and this is definitely the case with this divine dish. Many people use couscous instead of the traditional bulgar wheat but the real star of the show is, and should be, the parsley.

100 g/¾ cup bulgar wheat
250 g/9 oz. feta cheese, crumbled
2 shallots (or 1 small red onion), finely chopped
4 ripe tomatoes, chopped into 1-cm/½-inch pieces
2 bunches of fresh flatleaf parsley, finely chopped

1 small bunch of fresh mint, finely chopped
3 tablespoons olive oil
freshly squeezed juice of 2 lemons, or more to taste, plus the grated zest of 1 lemon
sea salt and ground black pepper

serves 6

Put the bulgar wheat in a shallow bowl and pour over enough cold water to cover. Leave for 20 minutes or so for the wheat to soften, then transfer to a sieve/strainer and rinse the wheat under cold running water until the water runs clear and all the starch is removed. Drain well.

Put the wheat in a large mixing bowl and mix well with a fork to separate any grains. Throw in the feta, chopped shallot, tomatoes (and any tomato juices released when chopping) and herbs and season well with salt and pepper.

In a separate small bowl, whisk together the olive oil and the lemon juice and zest. Taste this and add more lemon juice if it is not tart enough. Gently pour the dressing over the tabbouleh and mix really well.

480 ml/2 cups milk

2 eggs

110 g/1 stick butter, melted

375 g/3 cups plain/all-purpose flour

225 g/1½ cups cornmeal

1 teaspoon salt

4 teaspoons baking powder

110 g/½ cup plus 1 tablespoon sugar

1 x 198 g/7 oz. can (sweet)corn
kernels, drained (or use fresh corn
kernels cut straight from 2 corn
cobs/ears of corn)

a 6-hole muffin pan, lined with paper
muffin cases

serves 6

Cornbread with Mango Guacamole

In the USA, cornbread is one of those cowboy comfort foods that gets everyone smiling. Usually cooked in a cast iron skillet, this recipe sees the cornbread baked as savoury muffins, although you could always give the skillet option a go over a camp fire. You can also add loads of different accompaniments: Jalepeño chillies, Monterey Jack cheese or simply slathered in butter with a cup of coffee for breakfast.

Preheat the oven to 220°C (425°F) Gas 7.

In a large mixing bowl, whisk together the milk, eggs and melted butter.

In a separate large bowl, combine the flour, cornmeal, salt, baking powder and sugar. Make a well in the middle and slowly pour in the milk mixture, a little at a time, stirring until you have the consistency of a cake batter. Do not overmix otherwise the cornbread could come out a little tough. Lastly, stir through the (sweet)corn kernels.

Pour the dough mixture into the prepared muffin pan just to the top. Bake in the top of the preheated oven for about 20–25 minutes, until the cornbread is a deep golden colour and springy to touch.

Mango Guacamole

3 large ripe avocados

½ small red onion, finely chopped

1 mild red chilli, finely chopped

freshly squeezed juice of 1 lime

1 ripe mango, peeled, pitted and
chopped into chunks

a small handful of fresh coriander/
cilantro, roughly chopped

sea salt

serves 6

Cut the avocado in half lengthways, slicing around the pit. Holding one half of the avocado in each hand, twist your hands in opposite directions to open up the avocado. Dislodge the pit and discard it, then scoop the avocado flesh out into a mixing bowl and mash it with a fork. Add the onion, chilli and lime juice and mix well. Season with a pinch of salt, mix again and then gently stir in three quarters of the chopped mango and most of the chopped coriander/cilantro.

To serve, transfer the guacamole to a serving bowl and garnish with the remaining mango and the reserved sprinkling of chopped herbs.

150 ml/6 oz. Tennessee whiskey
  (Jack Daniel's No.7 or Jim Beam
  work well)
6 teaspoons muscovado/brown sugar
6 cloves
3 cinnamon sticks
freshly squeezed juice of 1 lemon
6 lemon slices, to garnish

a camping stove (optional)
6 tin mugs

serves 6

Cowboys' Hot Toddies

For a pleasant nightcap after a day on the beach and a sing-song around a driftwood fire, nothing compares to warming your hands and insides with a delicious hot toddy. There are many variations of the hot toddy; some use apple brandy and slices of apple, others say it's sacrilege if not made with malt whisky from the Highlands. But I really like this version. It may not help your lasso skills, but a cowboy hot toddy will certainly have you 'ye ha'-ing, if not perfecting the art of line-dancing before the night is out.

Put a pan of water on the camping stove or fire and bring to the boil. Swill a little of the boiling water around each mug to heat it up, then discard. Now add a 25 ml/1 oz. measure of whiskey and a teaspoon of brown sugar to each mug, along with a clove and half a cinnamon stick. Pour about 160 ml/⅔ cup hot water into each mug and, lastly, add a squeeze of lemon juice to each. Use the mug to warm your hands as the sun dips beyond the horizon and drink as soon as it is cool enough to do so.

Tip: If you aren't taking a camping stove with you, or having a campfire, you could make this up before you leave and pour into a thermos flask to keep warm, taking the cinnamon sticks and lemon separately to pop in the mugs as you serve.

Baked Banana Splits with Peanut Butter & Chocolate

When was the last time you had a banana split? Remember the days when splits were stuffed with all sorts of crazy accompaniments, such as glacé/candied cherries, sugar sprinkles, sweet whipped cream – and what about the sparklers!? There is something hugely nostalgic about this underrated kitsch dessert. This recipe combines four sweet ingredients that work beautifully together – chocolate, peanut butter, banana and cream. Believe me, banana splits never tasted so good!

Spray 6 squares of kitchen foil with oil.

Using a sharp knife, cut along the inner curve of each banana, about halfway through (enough to open the fruit rather like a book). Spoon a tablespoon of peanut butter into the crack of each banana and spread evenly before filling with chunks of milk and dark chocolate. Sprinkle a teaspoon of coconut over the top of each one, if using, then wrap each banana in it's own sheet of foil and pop in the cool bag along with a pot of whipped cream.

When you are ready to cook, place the bananas directly into the burning embers of the barbecue/grill and leave to cook for about 7–10 minutes. Remove from the heat and carefully unwrap the foil to check if the chocolate is melted and oozing. If so, serve with a dollop of thick cream on the side, otherwise return to the heat and cook for a little longer until the chocolate is molten.

cooking oil spray

6 ripe bananas, skin on

6 tablespoons crunchy peanut butter

50 g/1¾ oz. Swiss milk chocolate chunks

50 g/1¾ oz. plain chocolate chunks (70% cocoa solids)

6 teaspoons fresh grated or desiccated/shredded coconut (optional)

300 ml/1¼ cups double/heavy cream, whipped

a barbecue/grill

serves 6

Index

Stockists

Anorak
Online store, visit
www.anorakonline.co.uk
Style-driven products with a purpose; cooler bags, ground rugs and other essential picnic items with funky designs.

Baker + Bell
Online store, visit
www.bakerandbell.com
A fantastic range of picnic and glamping items featuring enamel and plastic tableware and outdoor cookware.

Cox & Cox
Online store, visit
www.coxandcox.co.uk
All the trimmings for outdoor living, parties and special occasions.

Crate and Barrel
To find a store or order online visit:www.crateandbarrel.com
Homeware store with a large selection of items for outdoor living, from plastic tableware to coolers.

Fortnum & Mason
181 Piccadilly
London W1A 1ER, UK
+44 (0)845 300 1707
www.fortnumandmason.com
The original luxury hamper store in the heart of London.

Lunchbox World
Online store, visit
+44 (0)7900 247998
www.lunchboxworld.co.uk
From food storage essentials to handy tips and hints.

Norton's USA
400 Lageschulte Street
Barrington, IL 60010, USA
+1 (888) 326-7997
www.nortonsusa.com
A uniquely American general store selling a large range of plastic and paper plates and servingware suitable for outdoor entertaining.

Not On The High Street
Online store, visit
www.notonthehighstreet.com
Stylish and fun items for outdoor living, weddings and parties.

Pedlars
To find a store or order online visit: www.pedlars.co.uk
Mail order, stores and pop-up shops selling quirky accessories for the great outdoors.

Picnicshop
Online store, visit
www.picnicshop.co.uk
A one-stop-online-shop for picnic hampers, bags, rugs and coolers.

Picnic Time
5131 Maureen Lane
Moorpark, CA 9302, USA
+1 (888) 742-6429
www.picnictime.com
A shop with all the brands you know and love for picnicking.

Sparks Yard
18 Tarrant Street
Arundel
West Sussex BN18 9DJ, UK
+44 (0)1903 885588
www.sparksyard.com
A place full of desirable things with an outdoors and seasonal edge.

Talking Tables
Online store, visit
www.talkingtables.co.uk
A huge selection of paper tableware including plates, napkins and cake stands, as well as decorative bunting.

Toast
Online and mail order, visit
www.toast.co.uk
Beautiful clothing, homeware and interesting items for the great outdoors.

Acknowledgments

I must first and foremost thank my mother for always feeding me good honest grub from day dot. Her food is like none other, and her table is always full of people wanting to eat it.

I must also thank Rebecca Woods and all the team at RPS for offering me the opportunity to write this book.

It's funny how the old adage of 'when one door shuts another one opens' holds true. Writing a book all about entertaining outdoors has been a dream of mine – it is wonderful to see that now a reality.

Lastly, but by no means least, I must thank my better half, Ross, for sharing my table and being my rock.